REVIEWS OF STEV
POSTERBOY FOR PLA)

MW00873460

Lynzee Klingman - Film Editor
Film editor of Hearts and Minds, One Flew Over the Cuckoo's Nest, A River Runs Through It, Man on the Moon. Your good nature, kind spirit and deep wit made these shorts and oh so sweet adventures with you engrossing, loving and deeply moving!! You have a unique voice in your writing, that is a blessed gift to you!! and the storytelling is a blessed gift to us.

Tom Benedek - Screenwriter, Cocoon, film-TV writing professor University of Massachusetts Amherst, University of Michigan, USC
"With vivid character detail and unexpected plot turns, Steve Sloane paints an illuminating self-portrait by artfully presenting his Great Neck childhood and beyond in memorable stories. From the kitchen of the Peter Pan Restaurant to a Sweet Sixteen Party through to adulthood, the stories are true, honest, and rich in human detail. Steve remembers the big things and so many little things that matter just as much."

Michael Sigman - Editor of Record World Magazine (1972-82) and Publisher of LA Weekly (1983-2002); author of many essays and three books about music and the music industry
Reading Steve's beautifully written, astonishingly detailed stories -- he remembers more than I ever knew about our high school days -- are a joy to read. They can also be simultaneously terrifying and hilarious, as in, "Ad's Hair Tricks", about a sadistic math teacher we shared with the initials GOD.
Fabulous piece!

Doctor Ronald Drucker - Author "Code of Life"
Steve, I read your short stories with anticipation and delight. Not only do they bring back vivid and poignant memories; but have both social and historical relevance. Your sense of humor, irony and insouciance is both refreshing and delightful; and very entertaining.

Richard Tabnick
Whoa! You should write a book!

Paulette Ballin

Oh my, Steve, this is terrific. I love your writing. Richard is right. You should write a book."

Jason David Wallach

Steve Sloane writes about real life, occasionally gritty with a discerning eye for telling details!

Shayna Stillman

Your stories are insightful, poignant and entertaining as you open your heart and mind to the reader. I'm so glad you are bringing your talent to a wider audience!

Linda Cahan

I look forward to reading your stories! They are well-written, evocative, always interesting and bring me to another place instantly.

Peter Gorin

Steve, I have thoroughly enjoyed reading your stories. Your style is very engaging, and I find myself drawn in almost at word one. Your attention to detail is great and makes the read and the ride that much more enjoyable. I look forward to seeing.

Robert Kogel

Why don't you write for the New Yorker?

Ellen Sara Firman

If your writing was a flavor, I'd be licking my chops! Love your stories. Always waiting for the next one!

Carol Nyhoff

I am enjoying this ride so much, Steve.

Muffin Friedman

Thank you, Steve for this wonderful tribute to your Mom.

Daria Vaccino

What a story!!!! Too bad it had to end!! Thank you for sharing!!!

Carol WohlI love this story!

Freda Simpson
That's a great story…can't decide if it is happy or sad.

Rick Sigler
You're rockin it!

Andy Topus
Wonderful stories. How do you do it? So descriptive and allegories throughout!

Betsy Shillinglaw
I thoroughly enjoyed this. Your storytelling is to the end of the world. Keep writing and sharing.

Nina Hanigsburg Richmond
I have thoroughly enjoyed your stories.

Ellen Siegel
I am swelling with love and appreciation about your contributions to the wellbeing of us all. From my heart and soul, thank you, Steve.

Marilyn Dydra-Breitgan
I get lost in your stories. Thank you.

Loren Green
I loved your story. This is a universal. Have you published?

Ellen Marcus
Great story. I am amazed how you remember so many details. I really enjoyed this. Please share more.

THE WRONG STUFF

By Steve Sloane

THE WRONG STUFF

By Steve Sloane

Copyright 2019

ISBN 9781729670026

CONTENTS:

Dedication
Acknowledgments
Author's Notes

Chapters:

Photos:
1) Cover - Music Class at Edgar Allen Poe School. Photo credit Steve Sloane
2) Paul Butterfield Blues Band at Café Au GoGo montage. Photo credit Steve Sloane
3) Year Book Photos of Dave Nash and Steve Sloane. Photo credit Kenneth Siegel
4) Party in Chinese Restaurant Kitchen. Photo credit Thomas Benedek

DEDICATION:

My grandfather, Zavel Carlinsky escaped from Bialystok when he was fourteen to avoid conscription in the Russian Army. He later gained American citizenship by serving as a "doughboy" soldier in World War I, rising to the rank of Mess Sergeant. He cooked for General Pershing's Army behind enemy lines in France. His German POW scullions scalded him. His experience in the war was so awful that he would not discuss it. He was an orthodox Jew but lost his faith in God.

In WWII, my father was drafted, and so was his brother. So were my mother's brothers, even those who were men in their thirties. My father was recruited by Wild Bill Donovan and served as an intelligence officer, undercover for the OSS, which was rare for a Jew. He spoke and wrote with respect about his military experience. His loyalty to our Presidents, our government and military were the subject of many angry and violent discussions in my home as the Vietnam War raged.

I grew up patriotic. I loved the movie, "Yankee Doodle Dandy" with James Cagney. I still do. I marched in the school band playing baritone horn and proudly wore the cap and sash given to me by the American Legion. "Over There", "It's A Grand Old Flag", and George M. Cohan's entire song book; I loved it. "America the Beautiful", "Star Spangled Banner", "Battle Hymn of the Republic", "Joshua Fit the Battle of Jericho", "When Johnny Comes Marching Home"; I love them all. I even led the Memorial Day Parade, as President of the interschool band when I was twelve. I was so proud. The formal uniform in the high school band in which I played starting in seventh grade had golden braids and epaulets on a fancy blue jacket. The trousers had gold piping too. Its hat had long feathered plumes. I marched and played John Phillip Souza's marches with all my heart.

My first doubts about this country had to do with prejudice towards Negroes and the anti-communist, black-list dirty politics of Joseph McCarthy. My parents were liberals. I attended a concert with Phil Ochs and was so impressed with his politics and music; including, "Too Many Martyrs", "The Draft Dodger Rag" and "I Ain't Marching Anymore", that I went to the music store and bought a guitar so that I could play and sing like him. I started then, in tenth grade and still love to play and sing his songs.

Buddhist Monks were burning themselves to protest war and that freaked me out. There was even a local college student named Bruce Mayrock who burned himself in front of the UN and died next to a plaque that quoted the Bible, "Let us beat our swords into plowshares." I was impressed. These martyrs cared so much that they gave up their lives. It strengthened my resolve to end war. I was a strong advocate of civil rights and joined the Civil Rights Club in my school. I found the militaristic aspects of band revolting and quit. Much as I loved the marches of John Philip Souza, I felt that my country was not genuine in its commitment to its highest ideals of truth, justice and freedom and that marching in the band glorified war.

As the Vietnam War escalated we saw atrocious images on TV every day. Our leaders were lying to us. Our country was killing innocent woman and children, farmers in their fields, burning their huts, poisoning their crops. My age was approaching eighteen, and as a high school drop-out, I realized that I might be called to serve. There was no way that I would go to Vietnam and fight against Ho Chi Min.

I had lost respect for Kennedy and Johnson. I never had any for Nixon. When Nixon was elected I burned my draft card and went underground. I left my wonderful girlfriend and carefree fun of adolescence behind me. This collection of stories chronicles those years, roughly 1965-1972. It is dedicated to every hero, coward, martyr, deserter, injured, maimed, guilty, ashamed, addicted, lionized or vilified, winner, loser, lost and forgotten, to every bad-luck soldier who abdicated his own free will and suffered the degradation, humiliation and failure of war.

ACKNOWLEDGEMENTS:

This book, "The Wrong Stuff" would have been beyond my skill set and not have gotten assembled, and published without the assistance of my crackerjack tech team, Karen and Avi Wolf. They also did all the tech work for my first book, "Posterboy for Planned Parenthood and Other Stories"; a perfect first take. Karen's patience and Avi's expertise were essential. Their kindness and sense of humor, friendship and affection, made the hardest parts tolerable and, at times downright fun.

Rose Hirschhorn taught me to read when I was eleven. It was an awful experience for me, but the magic moment came when she showed me the NY Times through a mirror. She is long gone, but her gift keeps giving. I read the Times every day. Its right wing editorial bias is so twisted that it must be written though a mirror.

My father was proud of his short tenures at the NY Times as a business reporter, before and after World War II. He was an excellent writer and I plan to reissue his book of short stories, "It's Been Charming as Hell". We shared an office for nine years and often read letters to each other and to Shirley, our brilliant office manager and at one time translator and editor for the Yiddish Forwards. She was also my office mother for twenty-six years and kept me on allowance until I was thirty-two. I had no idea what expert tutorial training I was receiving in writing, editing and comedy. Burt died a few years ago, and Shirley just this winter. I treasure the memories, and feel them when I write.

Better late than never to thank the girls I went to Junior High School with who passed notes that required me to respond. It was the first pleasurable experience I recall with written language. Thank you, Iris, Dorothy, Liz. We were so witty. What fun.

To my poetry reading fan club in tenth grade, Liz, Alisa, and Rona, AKA "The Troika", AKA "Steve Sloane Fan Club", thanks for providing grist for my pleasant reveries of sexual awakening, and for appreciating by budding talent. My patricidal verse was prescient, way before the offensive rap to which today's youths are enthralled. Thank you for listening, reading, and stroking my ego.

Collaborating with Moogy Klingman and Dave Nash helped me deepen my appreciation for the creative process. They both died too young, but I have to thank them, for their friendship, love, and continuing inspiration.

My friend, roommate and psychedelic guide Joe is one of those characters that is nearly beyond description. In this book he is a supporting character but he deserves a book of his own and I hope he writes it. He is a writer, and a wonderful friend in so many ways. He is a born leader, charismatic, iconoclastic, fearless, handsome, athletic and so good at so many things. His friends love him and I am grateful to be among them.

Lenny Bruce's favorite comedian was an aluminum siding salesman. He wasn't a professional comedian, but was the funniest guy he knew. I remember that when I think about my friend Crazylegs. His comedy was situational, physical, political and confrontational. Without formal training, he was a one man Living Theater, as in Julian Beck's troupe. Our collaboration was at times just friends having fun, enjoying each other's companionship, but there was another high energy component. We were political activists. Although we danced together and goofed together he brought a great sense of political theater, and the nerve to pull off some memorable hijinks. Heaven knows, we had our fun and it was sometimes for a good cause.

My wife Melanie is herself a veteran of Woodstock with a strong sense of justice and a deep appreciation for peace, love and understanding. She has read all my stories. Her patience and love have allowed me to devote myself to writing. Lucky for us she is studious and enjoys the time I am writing with reading and studying projects of her own. She has allowed me, in these mature years to be more introverted and literate, supporting me in all my eccentric habits, and sharing a life that becomes fuller and more loving every day.

I have been open and honest with my daughters and I think about them when I consider the subjects and what discretion I show in revealing my own character. I want them to know me and someday I want their children to know me too. So I have tried to be myself as truly as I can. Somehow they have accepted me and taught me along the way to be a good father. I have learned to love them more than I realized was possible. They are wonderful women and remain my continuing inspiration.

In editing this book I realized that my old friends and lovers were more valuable to me than my immature self could realize at the time. I have grown up since then, but still cannot fully acknowledge them here because not everybody wants their life to be an open book. I hope you are reading. The feelings were real. I wish I was more appreciative of the good things and more sensitive to your feelings. There are friends who I want to praise here but will not even mention to respect their privacy, but to you all, for the fun, the love, the adventure; thanks for everything.

AUTHOR'S NOTES:

In writing the Wrong Stuff I had to search my memory through all the layers of violence, trauma, alcohol, marijuana and psychedelic trips to find some order in a tumultuous time surrounding the War in Vietnam. It was not my intention to write a book, or to even write a story, or memoir. The writing actually started when my therapist asked me to write for her. Was it a dream, reverie, or some afterthought that our talk session stimulated? I don't remember that, but when I read it to her, she said, "You are a writer. Oh my God. Don't you know?" With her encouragement and more from my wife and writer's groups, I attempted to put some order in the most confused part of my life, forty years after. Now it is fifty years after. I have been writing for nearly fourteen years. Here, I have tried to make the story chronological and most of it is, but there is some overlap as flashbacks and recurrent themes have a way of disrupting time and making it irrelevant. So, I have taken license where necessary and abandoned time to let the stories fly.

Everything in the book is true except for the parts that I made up. The dialog is often made up in character. Is it true? Who knows? Is it accurate? I have gone to the sources and shared these stories when possible with the real characters on whom my literary characters are based. Some of my old friends have asked me to change the names and places, not out of shame or guilt, but to respect the privacy of their friends and family who might not want to have their good names and reputations associated with all the crazy and illegal things that we did and managed to survive. Others could not remember a thing. I have been amazed that old friends, who in some cases are smarter than me, can't remember better. Is it age or convenience? Maybe they just have better things to cram into their limited grey matter of memory cells. I would like to tell all the truth as I know it, but discretion got the best of me and I have tried to get the story across leaving many details to your imagination. Please feel free to project as much fun as you might imagine, regarding the sexual revolution. We didn't miss much.

The truth is still my highest value and writing it has been self-revelatory. I believe it is worth sharing. My political and social analysis that I developed while coming of age in the sixties still stands up. I was provocative in expressing my thoughts and caused personal violence. More than one set of hands has been around my throat trying to choke me for telling the truth and for asking uncomfortable questions. I have ducked many fists and caught a few. I have given some of that back. Now that I am older and wiser, I regret hurting anyone, with my words and fists. I wish I could have been more like Jesus. I am still trying to be a better man. My point of view seemed at once naïve and cynical to some, and theirs seemed just as wrong to me. They were so ignorant. There were times when I was overwhelmed and my deepest doubts seemed paranoid. I felt isolated by my politics. I still do. People suggested that I move to Russia or Cuba. Maybe I should have. Canada might have been a good choice, but I was committed to fighting for my values at home. How could our government be so venal and self-destructive as I believed and asserted? Was it just too sick for a sane mind to conceive? Thank goodness for Wiki-leaks, Chelsea Manning and Julian Assange. We were not paranoid. I did have some friends who agreed with me. It wasn't just our sick thoughts. Our government really has been as bad as we feared, and now we are even more aware. Some of us are. Some of us still prefer to punish the whistle-blower, kill the messenger and maintain incumbent values. My hope is that people will read this book, enjoy my adventures during the psychedelic age and develop insight into what happened to us, as a generation and as a culture.

PORTRAIT OF THE AUTHOR AS A YOUNG TROUBLE MAKER WITH STRAIGHT HAIR 1965

MUSIC CLASS AT EDGAR ALLEN POE SCHOOL
SPRING 1966

Here we are with the School's front door behind us at 24 West 74th Street. There were so many special schools on our block that we called it "Retard Row".

Left to right: Johnny Bumblebee, Fritzi Hall, the prettiest and shyest girl in school is hiding behind Zack, Zack, Ricky, Captain Moogy Klingman, Bird, Chuck, Maurice and Tony, The Commander of the HMS Pinafore. Photo credit, Steve Sloane

"So let it be written. So let it be done."
Pharaoh Ramses III in Cecille B. DeMille's "The Ten Commandments"

EDGAR ALLAN POE SCHOOL

Edgar Allan Poe School for underachieving, gifted and emotionally disturbed students was the last resort for one hundred and one of New York's brightest youths, who in 1966 were leaning towards the latter side of the qualifying equation. All of us had dropped out or been expelled from other educational institutions.

For some EAPS was the feeder for Riker's Island City Jail and/or Belleview's psycho ward. Belleview's portfolio of treatments included forced medication, electro-convulsive therapy and/or lobotomy. Ice-pick lobotomy was still legal and popular. Those among us who were initiated into the ranks at Riker's, usually for victimless crimes like possession of marijuana were abused, beaten and raped, which was par for that course. Such soul-numbing brutality was too often the precursor for suicide. For those who failed at that endeavor, it was a free feed into Belleview where we could meet former classmates in therapy but might not recognize each other anymore.

Not just anybody could get into this special school. Prerequisites included a high IQ and recommendation from a psychiatrist. As a qualified sixteen year-old drop-out, EAPS was suggested by my shrink. He said it was a progressive school along the lines of Summerhill with no attendance taken, no curriculum required, no homework assigned and no grades given. What was not to like?

Greeting Committee:

As a new kid, I walked unannounced into a birthday party for a Greek girl with a mustache named Ronni. The activity room was decorated with colored balloons and crepe paper. Nick Rapture and Rupert Hammer greeted me. Nick was a large pink-skinned youth. His strawberry blond hair was cropped close and flat-topped, with a pompadour that flipped with a spiral and fell over his feathery right eye brow. Wearing a tight dark suit and skinny black tie, he sat on the edge of a large Parsons table where some cake and soda were set up for a birthday treat. Standing at his side was Hammer, his best friend and henchman. He had an Elvis hairdo including low black sideburns. His slow-eyed face complimented his more flamboyant pal.

As I reached for a pretzel on the table, Nick spoke up with an edgy voice.

"You the new kid?"

"Yeah. I'm new."

Nick was smoking a cigarette. He raised it up to the decorations and popped a balloon. Then he raised his eyebrows, pursed his lips, and looked at me askance. "Smoke?" he said, snapping open a golden cigarette case.

"Thanks." I said. I took a Salem. Hammer lit me up with an enormous flame from his Zippo lighter. "Thanks." I said to Hammer. He withdrew without reply except to snap his lighter shut.

"You know Ronni?" Nick Rapture said to me.

"No. Who is he?

"Ronni isn't a 'he'. That's Ronni." Nick pointed with his chin towards a teenage girl with lumpy figure, oily, straight mouse-brown hair, pimpled skin, and a bit of a moustache.

"You think Ronni's a man?"

"I guess not."

"You guess not. Hammer. You hear that? 'I guess not'."

His sarcasm was malicious.

"Ronni is my friend and I don't think she would like to know that you think she looks like a man. I think that would hurt her feelings."

Rapture was getting on my nerves. I took a drag from the cigarette and popped a balloon with it.

"That is Ronni's balloon."

"So?"

I walked away and noticed that I was being followed by Nick and Hammer. When I got into the hallway, Nick grabbed my shoulder and I turned around. He blew smoke in my face and flung his cigarette into my chest. Then Hammer leaned into me, blew smoke in my face and threw his cigarette at me too. It bounced off my right cheek, just below the eye. My heart pounded with fear. It intensified when Hammer pulled a switch blade from his boot and sprung it open, close to my nose. I froze as he savored the moment. He had his neck twisted an eighth turn and his head down. With just one eye, he vogued at me, like James Dean.

I spun away in a crouch and ran down the foot-worn, five-flight, white marble, spiraled staircase, three steps at a time, with four steel-tapped boots clicking behind me. The percussion echoed into strange syncopation that reminded me of the drum solo in "Wipeout". I burst

3

through the front door outside onto West 74th Street. Sprinting west to Broadway, I turned left and downtown passing some junkies lounging on benches, enjoying low winter sun. I scrambled into the 72nd St. Subway Station, running down two steep flights of stairs, vaulting the turnstiles and got into a waiting CC downtown local train. The doors couldn't close soon enough to leave Rapture and Hammer behind. When the train started moving, I thought that I had lost their tail, but they opened the door between cars and chased me through the next car and continued their pursuit through several more. I jostled straphangers and annoyed readers who were sitting as disinterested witnesses to my peril. Nobody helped, except for a blind pan-handler who stumbled behind me and got knocked down. He shouted, "Motherfucker." He slowed them down. I wonder if anybody helped him. The chase continued through the train all the way to 59th Street Station where I jumped off and lost them when I switched to an available "A" train on its way to Times Square.

With Rapture and Hammer waiting for me the next day, I knew that I needed to make new friends.

Math:

In Math Class Mrs. P stood at the blackboard and tried to teach Trigonometry. I sat next to the "Z-man" who was 6'4' with a rosy-cheeked baby face. He was folding notebook sheets into paper planes. His gliders looked common, but when he flicked his wrist to launch them they flew like they had remote control; following courses and hitting targets.

Wally had a serious look about his goateed face. He appeared to be concentrating hard, hanging on every word from Mrs. P's lesson.

4

"Class. I am going to tell you how to find the square root of the hypotenuse in a right triangle."

This was too stimulating for Wally. He broke into the lecture.

"Tell me. Tell me. Tell me."

"OK, Wally. Give me a chance and I will tell you."

"Tell me. Tell me. Tell me."

Ray came into class wearing a nasty scowl and his varsity jacket. He was the star on our city championship basketball team. He had a black cloud over his head on this day. He sat in front of me and opened a large illustrated book titled "Black Rage". He ignored the class and concentrated on his reading. His book was illustrated with full page photos of flaming ghettos. He was gripping the sides of his desk so hard that it was making me nervous. I looked up from watching Ray's tight grip on the desk and saw Z-man watching it too. His childish eyes looked wet, like he was about to cry.

"David (Mrs. P didn't call him "Z-man"), are you paying attention to me? I am not paid to stand up here and talk to myself. I would appreciate it if everyone in this class would stop what they are doing and look at me while I am teaching trigonometry.

Raymond. Raymond Cochran. Welcome to class, Mr. Cochran. Good afternoon, sir. It is nice to have you present today. Do you think that you could take your face out of that book and look at me while I am talking to you?"

Ray looked up and said nothing. Then he looked down again and resumed his tan- knuckled scholarship.

Hector was alert as usual. He wore a plastic penholder inside his short-sleeve white shirt pocket which had no pens. He was a short and stout with big, shiny black glasses, like the abusive comedian, Jack E. Leonard. Thick lenses magnified his intense dark eyes which were twisted with astigmatism. He sat behind Penelope who had long straight brown hair. She was a plain looking girl of sixteen with a mouthful of stainless steel braces and a blank facial expression. Her adolescent figure had not yet formed curves, but Hector felt that her fresh cream rinsed hair was too attractive to ignore and he could not resist pulling it.

"Stop it!" She said.

"OK. What is the matter Penelope?" said Mrs. P.

"He's bothering me. He keeps pulling my hair."

"Hector. Why are you bothering Penelope?"

"I am not bothering her. She just wants to get me into trouble."

Z-man launched a glider. It flew high up near the fluorescent fixtures. Except for Ray, we all watched the paper plane loop the loop and then slalom down turning at the last minute to stick its point into Ray's left ear!

"Direct hit." said Z-man.

Hector laughed like a machine gun, "HaHaHaHa!"

Wally said, "Wooooh! Woooh!"

Zman started giggling and dribbling, shaking his head back and forth and wiping bubbly dribble off his mouth with the sleeve of his white shirt. He said it again, "Direct hit."

Ray got right up, walked to Zman's desk and punched him straight in the jaw. Zman's glasses went flying, as he was knocked out of his chair and fell back down in it slumped with a trickle of blood leaking out of the

6

side of his mouth. Zman was silent at first, from shock, and then started crying in a high-pitched whimper. Mrs. P reached him and started hugging and consoling him as he sat crumpled in his seat. She leaned her short body into him and patted his bloody mouth with a tissue.

Mrs. P said to Ray: "Raymond Cochran! You have a lot of nerve. You know the rule. No hitting, ever. I am so disappointed in you. You know better. You are really a very nice young man. You can behave much, much better than this. You hurt David. You have no right to do that. I don't think that you realize your own strength. What on earth got into you?"

"He threw his airplane at me! Why are you yelling at me? Why don't you yell at the Zman? I told him last time that if he hit me again with his motherfucking airplane I would knock his head off his skinny little babyboy neck."

"Ray. We do not hit. Come here and tell David that you are sorry."

"I am sorry. OK?"

"Come here and tell David you are sorry. Look at him. You hurt him very badly. Did he hurt you?"

"Oh come on, Mrs. P. I said I'm sorry."

"Come over here, Ray. Come here and say that you are sorry to David. You hurt him. I want you two young men to shake hands like gentlemen."

David's crying had subsided to mild sobbing. Ray came over and his mood was better than it was when he entered the class. Was it the physical release of hitting Zman, or was it the caring attention that he was receiving from Mrs. P? The more they talked, the warmer the relationship seemed.

7

Ray put his arms around our teacher and started talking to her like he was making up with a lover after a stormy fight.

"Ray! What are you doing?"

"Oh. I'm sorry Mrs. P. I didn't want to hurt nobody. My mamma doesn't love me enough. You're so nice to me. I don't want to let you down. I'm so sorry." Ray was holding her close and pressing his body into hers.

"Ray. This is very nice. You know that I think you are a wonderful young man. But don't you think that it is David that you owe the apology to?"

Ray had is arms around the diminutive and frizzy haired teacher and he was squeezing her, swaying and slow dancing to a spontaneous song.

"Oh, Mamma, you so nice to Ray."

"Ray. That is enough!"

"Come on Momma."

"Ray. This is really getting to be too much

It was enough for Hector. While we were watching Ray and Mrs. P, He took out his Zippo and lit Penelope's split ends. Penelope screamed and Hector laughed like a machine gun, "HaHaHaHa!"

Mrs. P. sprung to action and threw her cardigan sweater around Penelope's hair to smother the flames, but the damage was done. Hector was laughing and Penelope was screaming when help arrived in the form of Mr. Lubrecht, Mr. Hyman and Mrs. Hyman who owned the school. Hector was taken away and never returned. Penelope returned after about a week with a new shorter hair-style and a cool black beret.

Music Appreciation:

Music was more fun. We had a piano and a set of drums. Pete Cicero was sitting at the drums playing a sexy jazz beat. His ambition was to accompany strippers at the Metropole on 46th Street.

The rest of the class wandered in. Bird wore Carnaby Street fashions, like the Beatles. He was 6'6" and skinny. His straight brown hair hung near to his shoulders. His gap-toothed smile was goofy.

Ronny, not the girl, was an opera fanatic. He was a big clean-cut boy whose white shirt was always wrinkled and untucked. He could play the piano and sing the entire Gilbert and Sullivan catalog.

Johnny was a chubby boy who dressed like Detective Columbo. Behind his crooked, dirt streaked glasses he had a furtive look that suggested he might be hiding something under his trench coat. He was a concert pianist, who was competing for a big prize and aspired to be the next Van Cliburn but he only played one song, "The Flight of the Bumble Bee". Imagine it on piano.

I don't know why Ricky was in our class. I guess he liked music, but he was just a straight-ahead drug dealer. He was neither a beatnik, nor a hippy. Maybe he was some kind of hipster, but he just seemed like a young punk gangster. He pulled up in front of school and opened up the trunk of his SuperSport and it was full of drugs. There were two cardinal rules at EAPS:

1) No Drugs; we weren't even allowed to talk about drugs.
2) No Sex; we were not allowed to have sex in school.

These rules were not enforceable, but we all knew about them.

Rich Wakeskin was in music class too. He was a professional alligator wrestler and appeared on TV's "Wide World of Sports". He toured the world exhibiting his special ability to open and close Alligators' mouths and then to rub their bellies and put them to sleep.

His mother was a casting agent and he knew showgirls. Posters for the hit show "Golden Boy" showed Sammy Davis, Junior, the star with three beautiful women, a Negro, an Asian, and a Blond. One day, I was hanging around the entrance on 74th Street when Rich showed up driven to school in an impossibly small sports car full of those girls. He got out of the car tucking in his clothes and it looked like he was leaving an orgy.

Rich always looked the same, with eyebrows arched, jaw-dropped and panting. He wore his shirts opened to his belt with lots of golden jewelry hanging down onto his hairy chest. One day I went to the boy's room, and Rich was taming Gertie on a raincoat laid out on the tile floor. I never would have guessed that Gertie was so hot, but with Rich she was wild. I saw him in the same situation with other girls. He seemed to have what we called "the knack".

Billy Lionel:

Billy Lionel was in music class too. He thought he was a train. He wore goggles to protect his conjunctivitis from the fresh air. His eyes were runny and creepy looking. His expression was otherwise wide-eyed and too earnest. He wore a striped engineer's hat and walked with his bent elbows cranking in circles by his sides. He knew every train schedule and every stop in Metro NY. He seemed to know every train engineer. I observed him on more than one occasion involved in conversations with subway conductors.

At lunch time, Billy took orders, gathered and delivered. When he returned we had to treat him like the mail train. We would stand on the sidewalk with our hand stretched out like a hook, so that when the mail train went by, we could snag food.

Billy's sport was chopping wood. His family had a farm in Vermont and that is where he did most of his chopping. He often went there on weekends to work off his adolescent energy. He also walked across Central Park every morning from his apartment on 5th Avenue, churning and chugging.

Drivers' Education:

Billy was in the car sitting behind me in Drivers' Education on our first day. I had never driven before, except for the time when I was thirteen and Danny Lieberman showed me how to drive the 1949 Ford in his backyard. When I popped the clutch, the car lurched in reverse and crashed into the stucco wall, knocking plaster off inside the living room. His family was nice and did not report my accident.

Mr. Dick, our Drivers' Ed teacher, however, did not know about that incident, and had lots of confidence in me to operate our late model Chevy Nova sedan. We sat outside the garage on 100th Street just west of Amsterdam Avenue. The instructor used the precise jargon peculiar to his trade. He said, "Engage the key. Turn over the ignition. Release the parking brake. Shift the automatic transmission into "drive". Indicating a left turn with the electric signal flasher, I entered the flow of traffic. We did a bit of driving around the neighborhood, secure with the instructor in charge of the auxiliary controls, just in case an assist was required to avoid or navigate through an emergency. I tried to follow directions safely. What could go wrong?

We were traveling down Columbus Avenue with the west side of the Museum of Natural History on our left. Two youths whom Billy spotted and identified as Puerto Rican bicycle thieves were gaining on us from the shoulder riding fancy racing bicycles. As Jimmy stammered a warning, Mr. Dick said, "Using the directional signal flasher, indicate a left turn and execute the maneuver at the next intersection." I turned on the flasher but did not want to cause an accident with the cyclists and balked. As the intersection drew closer, Jimmy tried to spit out his warning but stuttered as Mr. Dick repeated his instruction with authority. I made a left. Unfortunately the bikers crashed into the back door, right where Jimmy was sitting. "Wa, wa, wa, watch out!" said Jimmy and then, "whammo!" One of the racers lost his balance. He way lying on his back sprawled out in the gutter, next to his bike. Thank goodness, he did not get run over. I followed instructions and pulled up to the curb on the next block. We observed the boy getting up and getting on to his bicycle, and riding with his friend around the corner on 77nd Street, toward Central Park. They seemed to be in a hurry. Billy said, "They are getting away!"

Mr. Dick said to me, "That does it. Don't you ever come back to this class, again. I will give you your blue card at the end of the semester and you can let your parents take you out driving until you are good enough to pass."

"But I told you I didn't know how to drive."

"Get in the backseat."

"You're the one who said to make a left turn."

"Get in back."

"But it was really your fault, Mr. Dick."

"Switch seats with Billy now or you can walk back to school."

I thought it was unfair, but gave up and followed his orders.

It was Billy's turn. He was signaling to enter traffic and was being extra cautious. Mr. Dick was unsettled from our experience and impatient. "OK, Billy. Stop stalling and start driving."

Billy continued to watch cars go by. Mr. Dick said, "OK, Billy. Enter the stream of traffic right now. It is safe. Go now. Billy, what the hell is the matter with you? Are you alright?"

Billy responded to Dick's urging by pulling his head back into the car. He turned his head and faced each of us to say his bit. It was profound. "You can be right, dead right."

I was still pissed off when I showed up for the lecture class a few days later. Dick called me out in front of the whole class. "Let's be clear. You are not driving with us anymore, so don't show up at the garage. You can come to class, but that is not even necessary. You can do the assignments but they won't count so don't even show them to me."

Telling me off like this was unfair. He had handed out pencils for our work-book practice tests, so I ceremoniously broke mine to punctuate his recrimination. Dick said, "What exactly do you think you are doing?" Without a word, a fellow student passed me another pencil. I stared at Dick, broke the second pencil and walked out of class.

Music, Music, Music:

Music class was better. I had a real problem with authority and generally hated adults, especially teachers, but our music teacher, Zack, was OK. He didn't seem to have a sense of authority. He was just another crazy boy. He loved pipe organs and traveled all over the world to play them. He was great at interpreting Bach and Beethoven. He demonstrated his prowess by taking us on a field trip to the Church of St. Peter the Divine up on Riverside Drive. The organ there was huge, like the instrument in the movie version of "Phantom of the Opera" with Claude Rains. This was world class!

Zack amazed us. He was great. I was impressed further that he was a Christian Scientist and did not take any inoculations. I hated needles too and admired him for refusing. I wished that I had been brought up Christian Scientist so that I could have skipped all the shots I got when I was a kid from mean old Dr. Siegel, the kid-hurting prick.

Every time Zack took summer vacation in a foreign land, he was put up in a hotel courtesy of the US Government and quarantined for a couple of weeks. He loved it and I admired that too. He lived in a back-room of a store in Times Square called "Tie-City". What a cool guy! He was gentle too and always seemed happy and smiley. He had a blond flat-top hair style, wore tight fitted suits with skinny ties. His slacks were tapered and short enough to show white socks, like spats.

When Zack entered the room the drumming was already rocking and he would watch and listen as though the drumming was going to stop out of respect for our class. After the rest of us entered, Zack would go up to the drummer and try quieting him down. He would hold the symbol between

14

his thumb and fingers to dampen the sizzle. He would press the heel of his hand on the tom-tom to dull the sound and even grab the sticks to make the music stop. All this was done with good humor and even the persistent drummer played the game with sportsmanship. Years later when I saw Pee Wee Herman on TV, Pee Wee reminded me of Zack. His good cheer was irrepressible.

Our drummer was not the only show-off in the group. As soon as the drumming stopped, Bob was likely to start playing "Flight of the Bumblebee" on the piano until Zack would close the key cover on his fingers to stop him. I was fond of playing my Hohner Marine Band Harmonica. Bird enjoyed sitting on the fire escape and playing the guitar. We played Delta style blues like Sonny Terry and Brownie Magee. Sometimes Ronny would get to the piano and start a Gilbert and Sullivan medley. The overall effect was chaos.

Trying to give the class some structure, Zack went to the stereo and put on a recording of the William Tell Overture. We found this stimulating and overpowering at high volume. We had little desks that were attached to the chairs, so we rocked and rode them around the room like carrousel horses. This was the scene when Zack convened class. We often turned on William Tell before he even arrived, because we loved it so much.

One day, Billy Lionel came unhinged during the pandemonium and went to the hall where an ax was kept behind glass with an instructional sign that read:

"In Case of Emergency, Break Glass"

Billy followed the written directions. He broke the glass, and took the ax. He chopped up the hall and bannister for a while. Then he came into the music room and started chopping everything in sight. We musicians safely evacuated. Billy was taken away and I never saw him again.

Abraham Lincoln's Birthday Annual Memorial Civil Rights Club Fund Raising Concert:

As the winter progressed I was joined at EAPS by my old pal and collaborator, Moogy Klingman, but before that, I had gone back to Big Egg High school to appear with his "Heebee Jeebee Jug Band" at the Annual Memorial Abraham Lincoln's Birthday Civil Rights Club Fund Raising Concert. I was introduced as a special guest and made my appearance from the audience.

"That's right folks." Moogy said. "We have a special guest tonight. He used to go to this school, but he left us a while back. He is very committed to civil rights and he has graciously agreed to come back here just for one night and join us up here on the stage to do his special signature dance. Let's make sure to let him know that we really appreciate him. His name is Saint Vitas and he is going to treat us all to The Saint Vitas Dance. So, let's give Saint Vitas a tremendous Big Egg High School welcome." I entered from the audience stumbling upon and bothering as many students as possible, while Moogy continued his introductions.

That was the same night that our shy friend, Andy Kaufman made his stage debut. Moogy introduced Andy. "We have another guest tonight who recently escaped from Communist Cuba. He is the fabulous blind Conga drum player, Pongo Loco. Let me bring Pongo Loco out here for your listening pleasure."

16

Moogy walked to the edge of the stage, leading him by the arm the same way that Billy Preston used to lead Ray Charles to the stage. Pongo was wearing big dark sun glasses and a Hawaiian shirt. He made himself comfortable behind a couple of Congo drums, next to the trap-set drummer towards the back of the stage.

Moogy started the band playing Muddy Water's classic Hoochie Coochie Man, and I started jiggling and twitching in my oversized suit. Many in the audience had been prepped to react to my dancing in the manner that defined euphoric fans of Elvis Presley and the Beatles. I wiggled and spazzed. I spun my tattered fedora on my index finger and launched it back-stage. I unbuttoned my loud hounds-tooth jacket. I took it off and swung it over my head. I threw it out to the audience which thrilled the kids who jumped up to catch it. My poetry loving fan-club called "The Troika" raved and screamed.

I went to the microphone and leaned in front of Moogy to say what Elvis would say, but in a meek foreign accented voice, because Saint Vitas was not an American, "Thank you. Thank you very much." That got a big laugh.

When I added James Brown splits and Mick Jagger struts, it ignited another wave of hysterics.

Again I approached Moogy and took the mike to add. "Thank you. Thank you very much." It was a running gag.

The jacket was overboard and so went the tie and big shirt. When I got down to my pants, I went behind the drums to take them off. Blind Pongo Loco turned towards me, raising his dark glasses with his forefinger to look. Then he turned around to the audience and raised his big black

17

eyebrows. That got a big bursts of laughter from audience before he dropped his dark shades back covering his eyes again.

To Al Nagel, the vice principal in charge of discipline, this was too provocative. He knew me and had helped pressure me to drop out of school the previous fall. To him, it was obvious that I was removing my baggy pleated trousers and preparing to do something obscene. He lowered the curtain fast and cut off the sound. Charles Perkel who had graduated and was a student at Bard, said "Fuck you," right in Nagel's face. Moogy was so mad that he went up to him and gave him the finger, point blank. It got him expelled. He soon turned up at Edgar Allen Poe School as my classmate.

You Gotta Have Friends:

When Moogy joined me, we spent lots of time jamming on our harmonicas. We experimented and found that the acoustics were excellent in the boy's rest room. Sometimes we jammed on the fire escape with Bird. We played in the hall and in the street. We were obsessed with playing our harmonicas. Moogy wanted me to drop out of school with him and start playing for tips in Greenwich Village. "Come on man. We can sweep floors, wash dishes, and play for tips. What are we waiting for?"

Moogy didn't have lunch money for John's luncheonette on Columbus Avenue. That's where some of us went to eat lunch, when Billy's train wasn't running. Moogy sat down as another customer got up, and he gobbled down their left over French fries, burger, and coleslaw. He even drank the leftover soda. He was scarfing down pickles and catsup when he was asked to leave. He took it as a political class-war insult, and

18

responded with Gorilla Theater, blowing his nose in a paper napkin and sticking it on the window when he got outside right where Rapture and Hammer were sitting in a booth eating club sandwiches. They could not tolerate uncouth and were not on his side of the political spectrum. They got up and chased him down the street and started a vendetta that lasted until spring.

Although Moogy and I were both Jews, Rapture and Hammer reserved Zieg Heil, for my fellow Hebrew. It looked like a Dr. Strangelovian Nazi reflex. Every time Rapture saw Moogy, he would give him a vigorous "Zieg Hiel" and a loyal "Hiel Hitler!" Sometimes it seemed theatrical, like theater of the ridiculous, or cruel. Hammer used his switchblade to menace Moogy, but never cut him. And Moogy had a reflex too. When he got the Zieg Hiel, he'd give the finger and say with clear defiance "Fuck you!" before leading another chase. Always the entertainer, Moogy would run like Charlie Chaplin, the Tramp.

As classmates, we all ran into each other in the music room and that is where we could sometimes put aside our mutual hatred to jam. Rapture played piano like Jerry Lee Lewis and he rocked hard singing,

"Jenny, Jenny, Jenny,

Won't you come along with me?

Jenny, Jenny

Woooo (in a delirious falsetto)

Jenny, Jenny…"

He pounded the keys and his face turned red when he sang. If he wasn't still a teenager I imagine that that kind of excitement might have given him a stroke. He put his steel-tapped, black boot up onto the keys and pounded his heel down. He ran the backs of his hands up and down on the keys like Liberace and screamed like a maniac.

After he finished he would get up on the bench and instead of bowing, he would give a Heil Hitler salute and start chasing Moogy.

Rapture had another reason to hate my friend. He was a piano player too and we only had one piano.

Maurice:

My friend Maurice played electric bass. He was a cool guy from the Bronx. He had a soft breathy baritone and always stayed calm. He used to say stuff like, "Hey Moogy. Come mea. How you doing? I saw you with your girl-friend. She's cute. Does she give? What's her number? Just kidding. No really, what's her number?"

While Maurice was talking to Moogy, Rapture and Hammer left him alone. It saved him from some serious hassling. For some reason they respected Maurice, or were repelled by the sex talk. Even though Maurice was 5' 6", he was the man, and no harm came to me or my friend when we were in his company.

English Literature:

Maurice was in a my English class and he liked the time that our teacher Mr. Lubrecht, who was also the baseball coach passed out some poetry books and told us what to read at home. Although we liked poetry and I was known to write some patricidal free verse of my own, we were adverse to homework. I put the books in a neat pile on my desk and lit them up with my Zippo. Lubrecht was writing on the chalk board and all eyes were on my fire, watching with growing admiration. It was a little fire that licked up the corners of the cloth bound books. We liked it. No homework was the rule and it needed to be enforced. We did not belong to a union, but we students all shared this self-interest against homework. We had suffered with it in other schools and we could not allow it to take hold at Edgar Allen Poe.

When Lubrecht turned around he ran over and pulled my books apart, scattering them on the floor so that he could stamp on the smaller individual fires, which kept him busy for a few minutes. The class laughed as the big man raised his hands above his head and stamped his feet which resembled the Mexican Hat Dance. I felt pretty cool until he grabbed me by the scruff of my neck and dragged me outside in the hall and down the stairs to the principal's office for an angry report.

Mr. Hyman called my shrink and sent me home. I was suspended indefinitely and I guess that I was lucky not to have been arrested or otherwise incarcerated. Dr. Steiner gave me a prescription for Valium starting me off with a free sample in his office. Valium was supposed to help me keep calm.

My parents were informed, but we did not have much to say that I can remember. There was no punishment. I had been out of their control for quite some time. I went to therapy with Dr. Steiner where I smoked hash and didn't say much. I didn't like the idea of a psychiatrist trying to control my mind and make me be an obedient boy. Next thing you know he'd have me joining the army and killing Vietnamese patriots. The valium reduced the buzz from the hash. I did not like it, but I took it as prescribed along with lots of alcohol which I got from an old guy named

Abe who hung around town with teenagers. A week later I went back to school, as if nothing had happened. Lubrecht didn't say another word, and we did not get any homework. What had he been thinking?

Even my worst behavior was not so bad in the context of my fellows. We had a guy named Glenn who on more than one occasion punched his fist through school windows and had to be rushed to the emergency ward for treatment. I know a girl who found that sort of self-destructive behavior to be romantic and irresistible. A psychotic episode was a status symbol. The world was sick. We were "unsane" and proud of it.

Play Ball:

Maurice and I both made the softball team that spring. Maurice played short-stop and I played second base. We were a terrific double play combination. I had lots of experience and coaching from playing Little League at camp and had been on a regional championship team. After I hit the ball over the left fielder's head a few times, I became popular, even with the Nazi Party and our coach, Mr. Lubrecht.

Maurice was completely competent at short and practically nothing got through the infield.

Rapture played first base. He was athletic and agile for a big boy, also a sadistic bastard. If he had the ball and a base runner was foolish enough to run to first base anyway, Rapture would make him sorry. He smacked base runners with the back of his mitt, sometimes right in the face. If that started a fight he liked it more. He enjoyed brawls as they gave him more cause to smack our competitors. The umpires intervened, but were ineffective in forging lasting peace.

At third base we had Freddy Serpico. He loved codeine cough medicine and beer for a chaser. He often kept a bottle of beer, just on the foul side of his bag. He did not change his clothes for softball like the other boys did. He wore Leonardo Strassi woven shirts with matching woolen covered buttons, tapered slacks and pointy leather shoes popularly called Puerto Rican fence climbers. Freddy was the steadiest, stillest athlete that ever played. He stood near the base and his beer and did not crouch or move. Still, somehow, every ground ball on the extreme left side of the infield bounced into his glove and every sizzling line drive hit his glove in the webbing and stuck there like it was magnetic. He didn't waste any motion and managed to step on the bag and throw runners out with no sweat.

In right field was my pal Big Train Henderson, who was no relation to Billy Lionel. I don't remember why I stared calling him Big Train. He was tall and skinny. His face looked just like early Bob Dylan, which in 1966 was the only Dylan there was. I am talking about the cover of Freewheeling Bob Dylan. Big Train was an electric guitar player and was thrilled when Dylan went electric too!

I enjoyed hanging out with Big Train and Eleanor the guidance counselor. We actually had some calm and pleasant games of five-hundred Rummy and Casino with Nick Rapture, who it turned out was a young man of many moods. Playing ball brought us together in peace even more than playing music. Big Train had a wistful and amused look and way about him that I found appealing. He was a good ball player. Eleanor was a Negro, and got along fine with Rapture. In her presence, he refrained from his Nazi histrionics.

23

In center field was Dave DeFoe who I did not get to know. He was a strapping handsome fellow, who kept to himself. He came from Montana and as I recall, he did not speak. They say that he hallucinated from heavy use of LSD and DMT which was added to marijuana for hallucinatory extra effects. Sometimes Dave would go running after the ball before it even left the pitcher's hand. We would look out to center field and Dave would be loping after an imaginary ball, preparing to make a game saving catch. Sometimes we had to halt play and go retrieve Dave, because the imaginary ball would be past the limits of our field. When he was paying attention to the real ball he was the most gifted athlete on the team. He could run fast and throw the ball really hard; sometimes too hard. One time he threw the ball all the way from left-center field over the batting cage and into the bleachers of the field on 81st Street and he hit a drunk and made him fall down about five rows. We thought it was a great throw and had a rowdy group laugh. The drunk got pissed off and his cursing made us laugh harder. He started throwing bottles and rocks and was headed out to the field to get DeFoe when our coach Mr. Lubrecht interceded.

Lots of seedy men sat around the bleachers drinking in the afternoon and watching us play. We often heard bottles breaking during the games and observed drunks fighting which added to the atmosphere of our national past time.

Hammer was our left fielder. He was all business. He caught everything and threw the ball into second hard. He also had a great peg to the plate and didn't like it when Maurice cut it off in the infield.

Our catcher Eddie was a tough fat Italian kid from Brooklyn who won the batting title hitting over seven-hundred.

It was a great year. During the first game against Walden, we lost 12 to 8, but we injured half their team. Rapture had a great game, by his own standards. After the game we hung out and got stoned with some of their guys who were in a band called "The Soul Survivors". They had a hit song called "Expressway to Your Heart". When they were show-cased at the Anderson Theater on 2nd Ave., we went to see them. They made a great entrance, swinging in onto the stage hanging off of ropes.

After that first game, we got a new pitcher named Bobby who could throw the ball past just about anybody. There were lots of ground balls and pop flies and we didn't lose any more games. We were ISAL champs (Institutional School Athletic League). At the awards ceremony, Willis Reed who played center for the Knicks gave me my trophy.

Looking for Love:

I didn't go to class much except to play music and softball. I often went to the zoo by myself to visit the Gorilla in the monkey house. He looked like a morose prisoner. Had he ever been wild? The little monkeys screamed and chattered, but he just stared at nothing with blank, blood-shot eyes. I couldn't tell if he focused on anything. His eyes were open, but what did he see? I wondered if he would like to smoke pot, but did not get that close. It smelled awful in the monkey house, and the fresh air and fun outside was much better. I especially enjoyed watching the seals swim and perform tricks for herring rewards.

Sometimes I wandered into seedy local bars and drank beer while cheesy looking women took off their clothes. Lenny Bruce was one of my idols. I was fascinated by the strippers and the men who watched them. They seemed so unhappy. I couldn't understand why something as great as sitting around watching women take off their clothes could be so depressing, so every time I found another bar with strippers, I would go in and hope for a better experience. They were pretty poor and I determined to get a girl-friend instead.

Maurice suggested that I go visit him in the Bronx to hang out on Pelham Parkway and pick up chicks. So I took the train up to visit him and meet his friends on Wallace Ave, near Bronx Park, which included the Bronx Zoo and Botanical Gardens. Maurice and his friends had a clubhouse in the basement of Greenberg's apartment house. It was decorated with Playboy Centerfolds and raunchier porno than I had ever before seen. We played music. Maurice who, during the summers was a working musician in the Catskills, playing at the Raleigh Hotel favored the Ventures, Jan and Dean and surfer music that was new to me. I enjoyed the groove and had a great time with him, sitting in on harp and fooling around on drums.

Later we ate pizza and checked out the local talent, which is a phrase that Maurice used for chicks. We hung out on the Parkway which is a broad boulevard like you might expect to find in Paris. It has lots of grass, benches, and trees in the middle of double-lanes. Between the boulevard and sidewalk, is a smaller road, then there is more grass and sidewalks, then lawns and stately brick apartment houses. We made our way west to the more commercial district and started checking out the girls.

"Hey. You're cute. What? No smile? Come on. Give us a smile. Bitch. Dyke." Maurice always knew just what to say.

Busted:

So we hung out and tried to attract girls. I did not think that this was a good location. The girls were not as cute as Manhattan or Big Egg where I came from, but we persisted until a paddy wagon came and stopped in front of us. Cops jumped out and busted us and about ten other guys for loitering. While they were loading us up, Maurice and I ran away.

We went around the corner and saw the Paddy Wagon stuck in traffic. Maurice started yelling at it.

"Hey Greenburg! Greenburg! Hey Greenburg!"

He whistled loudly like he was hailing a cab. Maurice ran up and knocked on the window where Greenburg was slouching. I followed.

"Hey, Greenberg!"

Greenburg turned around to see us. Maurice said, "Hey Greenburg! You suck! You're a schmuck!"

Greenburg couldn't understand what we were saying. He was cupping his hands by his ears and wrinkling his brow, shaking his head no.

Maurice said louder and more deliberately. "YOU ARE A SCHMUCK!"

Greenburg gave us the finger.

Maurice and I looked at each other and cracked up.

Skinny Girls Screw Easy:

Later that night we connected with Enid and Bernice. They had curlers and I would never look at them twice, but Maurice insisted that they were hot and that Enid liked me.

"Believe me. These girls give. Just act like you don't care, and they will do anything to get into your pants." We showed up at Enid's apartment to pick her up and her father answered the door. He was a burly, bald headed man wearing a sleeveless undershirt and drinking beer from a can.

"Hey, Enid, get out here."

We made nervous small talk and walked over to her friend Bernice's apartment. When we rang she just came downstairs to meet us. We walked to the Botanical Gardens which were still and dark. Maurice took Bernice's hand and looked back at me, so I took Enid's. Her hair was done in a bee-hive. Her tight jeans and dicky top showed off an attractive shape. We walked until Maurice stared making out with Bernice. He liked Bernice because she was skinny and flat with bad skin. Maurice had informed me with an axiom,

"Skinny girls screw easy."

He shared another secret about females that I had never thought about but that seemed to make strange sense. "That acne means that their hormones are going crazy and they are really hot and they need dick."

Enid turned to me. I noted that her heavy application of pancake makeup had made her skin eruptions invisible, but I could feel the magnetic attraction. Maurice was right. I gave her a kiss and she put her tongue in my mouth. It tasted minty but seemed unsanitary and I didn't like it. She was not discouraged. She pulled my head close and blew her warm breath slowly into my ears. It sounded like the ocean in a conch shell. She swirled in my ear with her tongue. I liked the blowing better than the tonguing. I won't share the details except to say that I found the experience satisfactory and soon we had ice cream cones to lick while we promenaded down the parkway holding hands. I entertained by walking in a crouch to hide the wet mark on my tan pants. Enid laughed hard and begged me to stop, but couldn't stop laughing, so I continued. The girls went one way and we went to Maurice's apartment still laughing about our dates.

Later that summer, Maurice came over to my house. I had told him I knew cute girls with nice skin and round figures that might be just as hot as the girls we met in the Bronx, so he called my bluff. It worked out so well, that I developed a relationship into a full blown teenage love affair with a girl that did not qualify at all, by Maurice's standards.

In the fall I went back to public school and lost touch with most of those crazy kids I knew from Edgar Allen Poe.

THE SCOOTERS

October rain tap-danced on the slate roof. Lightening flashed tall tree silhouettes in the garden and stroboscopic snap-shots of teenagers cavorting inside the house. Scotty and Marlene hugged, standing behind the couch. I pressed on Donna leaning over the back of a leather club chair. We were bold and awkward, struggling with elastic, turning our hips and straining our fingers to thrill private places. Thunder clapped and rumbled encouragement. Schlomo, the host and odd-man-out put a record on the stereo. Its music was so astonishing, that it stopped our sophomoric surges as our ears became our most vital organs.

"What instrument is that?" said I.

"Is it a French Horn?" said Marlene.

"Is it a saxophone?" said Scotty.

"Tenor sax?" said I. "Sonny Rollins?"

"It might be an amplified oboe," said Donna.

The girls started pulling their clothing back in place while the boys tucked their shirts into their trousers. "What is that sound?" I said again to everyone. "It is incredible!" The teenagers were digging the music, without knowing to whom credit was due.

Schlomo shed some light with the dimmer switch in the big glass chandelier. All five teenagers continued listening and danced crazy beatnik freestyle, with elements of twist, jerk, and bop. When the record ended, Schlomo told them that they had been listening to The Paul Butterfield Blues Band's "Born in Chicago". They had never heard of

Paul Butterfield before, but it was his electrified harmonica that made an indelible impression on them all, especially me.

I wanted to play harmonica. Saturday morning at Barrow's music store I bought a Hohner Marine Band in the key of "D" for $2.50. It was what Butterfield played.

There were some talented seniors at Big Egg High school. A few had already distinguished themselves playing "harp" as they called it in jug-bands which were popular in the acoustic days of 1965. My neighbor Gene Heimlich was a virtuoso. Although Gene had a caustic wit, he took a liking to me and gave brief impromptu lessons. Along with my blues loving buddy Moogy Klingman, I practiced often. Moogy and I prowled the halls playing cross-harp duets between classes. We lingered and violated scheduled grace periods playing harmonica concertos in the restrooms and stairwells. Tile-walled acoustics echoed and magnified our sounds. We annoyed our teachers and impressed our friends. At a jam session in Buckley Greengrass's basement, I got to the mike and started to play the blues accompanied by two electric guitars, bass, drums and a keyboard. The bent high notes from the harmonica's sixth hole were wailing and otherworldly. I could hardly believe that it was me. My tucka-tucka, double-tongued low-note rhythms gave the band power and depth. The amplification made it all sound so great, like Paul Butterfield! Electricity was the drug. I was hooked.

We decided to be a band and played the Paul Butterfield "Born in Chicago Album" over and over. I jotted down the lyrics. I was the singer and harmonica player. Doug was the lead guitar player. He had a phono-graphic memory and could copy the mind-blowing Mike Bloomfield lead guitar solos in one take. Dave played rhythm guitar, like Elvin Bishop on a gorgeous red Gibson hollow-body. Joel looked like Art Garfunkel and played keyboard much better than Mark Naftlan on the record. Bernie played bass. Ray played drums. Dave called the band "The Scooters" and it stuck.

That basement was always full of other music-loving teenagers. The Scooters, Rob Kogel and the Nighthawks, The Savages, Adam and the Edens all came to play. Anybody could pick up an instrument and jam. Some kids just listened and danced like minor-league groupies. Philosophical discussions were conducted upstairs with Dave's mother, Gert moderating. She was an artist and enjoyed hosting her son's friends. She was generous with food, drink and compliments. Gert let the kids have whatever they wanted and kvelled.

One night the Scooters loaded into my 1961 bronze colored Chrysler New Yorker. We headed into Greenwich Village to the Café Au Go Go to see The Paul Butterfield Blues Band. The turquoise green domed dashboard was glowing like neon as we boys smoked pot and listened to our idols on eight-track tape. Joel, sitting in back, on the right, cracked the electric window and stuck his tall nose out to avoid the fumes and breathe fresher air.

Entering the club downstairs on Bleeker Street, we got great seats up front so that we could observe the professionals' techniques. The band commanded the small stage and even tuning-up excited us.

"What is Butterfield doing to his harp, man?" I asked Dave.

"He dunked it in a glass of water."

"What is he, ah, like cleaning it?"

"Oh God. Geez. That's the way my grandmother washes her dentures." said Joel.

"Yich!"

"Don't worry, man. He's, ah, he's not going to drink it. He has a bottle of Jack Daniels, ah sitting on top the speaker," said Doug. "Let's see if the vibrations knock it down."

Bloomfield let a few licks fly. The power was on. We grabbed each other's arms and looked left and right at each other's faces with mouths agape. It was the thrill of a lifetime. When the band actually played their set, it was ecstasy for the packed house of fans. Bloomfield's electric single stringed guitar riffs, dipped and swooped, whirled and soared. It was great music; eccentric and inventive beyond belief. Butterfield's full rich tone on harp was real after all. His lyrical extended solos were complex and compelling. His rhythm was syncopated and strong. His singing was bold and full of heart. The band played the entire album that we had memorized.

Then we went across the street to The Bitter End Cafe to dig The Blues Project's great guitar player Danny Kalb with Al Kooper on keyboards. We ate greasy fries with catsup and drank cherry cokes, except for Joel who drank hot tea.

After that we went back to the Café Au Go Go for the last set. Promoters called this Bleeker Street double feature "The Blues Bag Jam". In fall of 1966, it was the start of a tradition. When the set was completed, we left our front row seats, took a few steps forward, and headed backstage, without hassle or complaint.

I had been snapping pictures of the band with a Canon 110mm half frame during the show. As my bandmates went ahead, I stopped Paul Butterfield himself in the hall and took a few pictures. While my idol posed for a portrait, I praised his music.

"Hey, Paul, you played great. I can't believe your tone is so big and fat. First time I heard your record I thought it was Sonny Rollins."

"Wow, Sonny Rollins. I don't think so man. He plays tenor."

"I know man. But you play so great. Is it really just a harp?"

"Yeah, man Marine Band. Some people like the Blues Harp, but I like the Marine Band. Can't beat it."

"Who did you learn from? Ah, I mean, ah who do you listen to?"

"Little Walter. He is it, baby. Can't beat Little Walter. He played with Muddy and Wolf. And Junior Wells. How 'bout you, man? You dig Little Walter?"

"I don't know if I ever heard him."

"If you heard Muddy and Wolf, you heard Little Walter. You dig Junior Wells, man?"

"I don't know?"

"Don't know Junior Wells? Don't know Little Walter? I guess you don't know Sonny Boy Williamson and Lightening Hopkins either."

"Not yet."

"Man. There's two Sonny Boy Williamson's, and they are both great."

"Really?"

"Yeah, man. I ain't lyin." He chuckled. "You got a lot to learn little brother."

"And your tone is so big. How do you get that big juicy sound?"

34

"I wet the reeds, man. I wet the reeds. It makes a richer tone and a deeper bend."

"How do you bend the single notes so deep?"

"Well, man, I kinda block the other holes with my tongue and lips and suck the air in like I'm smoking a tight joint. Like I'm toka, toka, token." He laughed. "You dig?" They were laughing at his onomatopoeic pun and looking right in each other's faces.

"I do. I do. Thanks, man. That's how I do it too. Seriously, man. Toka, toka, token?" I snapped a shot.

"Yeah, man. Well, that's alright," said Paul and I snapped another.

The rest of the Scooters were already backstage when I caught up. In the small green room they found the keyboard player, Mark Naftlan fooling around, relaxing and playing Bloomfield's guitar. Doug grabbed it and started playing.

"Hey kid, gimme back that guitar. That's Bloomfield's Les Paul. He'll kill you, man."

Doug just played it unplugged, evading Naftlan's reach, dancing backward with agility and making bluesy faces like we had just seen on stage.

The rest of us Scooters looked at each other and at Doug who never ceased to amaze us with his nerve and his talent.

Bloomfield entered the room and Doug went up to him and started playing his guitar right under his nose. Bloomfield looked down at Doug and Doug looked up at Bloomfield. Doug played the solo that Bloomfield had just played to end the show. As Bloomfield realized that he was listening to an exact replication of the solo that he had just invented, he shook his head and opened his mouth in amazement, nodding his head behind the beat, in recognition. He was in awe, of Doug and himself. It was all so great; the inspiration and the appreciation.

Bloomfield said "Wow, man. That is great. Where did you learn to play like that?"

"From you, man," said Doug, "from you." And he played another solo back, looking right at his idol and mimicking the faces that he made while he played on stage. These were the faces that we associate with the blues, like people's faces when they are approaching orgasm and having orgasm; like agony and ecstasy with contorting muscles and extreme emotions, like a mother in transition and giving birth.

"Wow man. That's great," said Bloomfield.

"Hey Mike," said Doug. Where did you learn to play like you do, man"

"Wow. Like did you ever listen to BB King, and Albert King, and Freddy King?" said Mike. "Hey, give me a paper and pencil. I'll tell you who to listen to."

We couldn't find any paper except for a crumpled brown sandwich bag that had some grease stains on it, and somebody gave Bloomfield a pencil. The point was blunt so he sharpened it with his thumb nail.

Joel and Dave were looking at each other with concern while Bloomfield cut wood with his nail. We all looked around at each other, because there was something about Mike.

"Do you ever listen to Albert King? He is such the best, man. You gotta listen to Albert King." Sitting on a beat-up broadcloth easy chair and leaning against its soft arm, Mike was scratching away on the bag with the pencil and smoothing the wrinkles on the bag with the heel of his hand. He had that same intensity with which he played the guitar. It is a lot of intensity. Even his hair looked electrified.

"Albert King," said Doug.

"Yeah, man. Do you dig Albert King? Born Under a Bad Sign? Cross Cut Saw? You gotta dig it man. It's the most."

"Yeah, thanks, Mike. Albert King." Doug played a few dead-on riffs from "Born Under a Bad Sign".

"And did I say BB King?"

"Yeah, man. BB King. He is cool." Doug replicated BB King's sound.

"And what about Freddy King? You know Freddy King?" said Mike as he wrote.

At this point I was wondering if I had smoked too much pot. First it was Butterfield and all the harmonica players with diminutive first names like "Little", "Junior", and "Sonny Boy"; Two "Sonny Boys" in fact. Now Mike Bloomfield had just recommended three great guitar players who all had the same last name. They were all "Kings" and I had never heard of any of them. Too many Kings for me, but really, as I would learn, not too many at all. They were all great. And they were all Kings; BB, Albert, and Freddy.

We went back to our seats and enjoyed the next extended set too, leaving the club at about 4AM.

Later in the car, as I drove, the other boys inspected Doug's paper bag souvenir, with the notes written by Mike Bloomfield. Joel commented,

"Geez. His penmanship, God, look at it, man. It looks like chicken scratch."

"And dig this bag," said Doug. "It looks like it was full of fried chicken. Do you think it could be any greasier?"

Mike Bloomfield had recently played lead guitar with Dylan at Newport in that famous concert wherein Dylan shocked the folk-music loving world by going electric. He played all the leads on Dylan's greatest of many great records and his first electric, the masterpiece "Highway 61 Revisited". Al Kooper, whom we had just seen playing keyboard with Blues Project was with Dylan and Bloomfield at Newport and on "Highway 61". With Bloomfield's riveting solo on "Devil with a Blue Dress", Mitch Rider and the Detroit Wheels went to the top of the charts. When we met him, Bloomfield was touring and on contract with Paul Butterfield and he was the hottest lead guitarist on the planet. Soon, when Mitch Rider asked him to tour with him, he could not, so he recommended Doug. Doug turned sixteen, took the job and toured the world.

Another musician from Big Egg High, Mike Lecovsky dropped out of his band, The Left Bank, which was famous for a song he wrote called "Walk Away Renee". Joel took over his job at keyboards and went on his way too.

Without Doug and Joel the Scooters disbanded and regrouped.

PHOTO MONTAGE OF PAUL BUTTERFIELD BLUES BAND AT CAFÉ AU GOGO: Billy Davenport on drums is a blur. Jerome Arnold on bass is singing. Paul is top and center pausing for an impromptu interview. "Toka, toka, tokin." Below left is Elvin Bishop. Lower center has Mark Naftlin standing next to Jerome and Elvin. Lower right is the hottest guitar player on planet, Mike Bloomfield. Photo credit Steve Sloane.

The producer of "Horn from the Heart", the Butterfield Biopic, told me that Paul Butterfield did not give interviews, which makes this photo and interview rare. Read it here. It's exclusive in "The Scooters".

THE GRADUATES

Dig It Do It

Steve and Dave graduated from High school on Wednesday morning. Like some of their fellow classmates at Big Egg High, during the ceremony they were naked under their caps and gowns. Nobody could see, but the naked knew. It was an anonymous expression. They were for civil rights, against the Vietnam War and conscription, for free love, and getting high on marijuana. Amoral, and unsane, they rejected dogma and artificial boundaries of conventional consciousness. They had figured life out. Hedonists, they were; "dig it, do it", was their credo. They received their diplomas as Jesse Colin Young and the Youngbloods sang "Come on people, smile on your brother, everybody get together and love on another, right now."

Later that day, Steve packed a suitcase and drove his maroon Peugeot 404 to Dave's stepmother's house. She was known as the wicked witch for good reason. She hated her step-son, Dave, who looked too much like her despised, ex-husband, Harry. Harry had divorced Dave's clairvoyant birthmother, Naomi when she had a nervous breakdown and was institutionalized. She lost custody of her little boys. Dave was just a toddler. His mother could neither take care of herself nor him and his elder brother. Harry took his boys and married the wicked witch. He promptly divorced her too (who could blame him?), and left the boys with the witch to raise them (who could forgive him?). Unfortunately for Dave, the witch had a big boy named Mark who enjoyed beating his little step-brother, pissing on him and locking him in the attic of their neat three-

40

floor colonial, far from loco parentis. The abuse and humiliation lasted for years. Dave was traumatized, suffering alone in secret shame. On graduation day, he didn't have a suitcase, so he ran downstairs with his clothes stuffed into a pillow case, ready for his great escape, and a cross-country drive.

"Well, um, a Dad…I, ah, um…Dad…so, um, a, Dad, well…we are leaving now." Dave informed his father, Harry who was sitting in a big chair with his head behind the Wall Street Journal. Harry was visiting the house that he funded with alimony and child-support. He visited to manage seasonal maintenance and collect his due from the bitter raven-haired beauty, known to children as "The Witch". Harry did not look up or say good-by. The boys walked out the front door.

"Good-bye, Mr. Nash." said Steve, over his shoulder, behind his right hand.

"Wise-guy." said Dave, under his breath.

Mr. Nash continued his oblivious demeanor. This caused the boys to burst out laughing as they cleared the front door stepping on the flagstones. Inside the car they could feel their freedom rising and their laughter lost its restraints.

"What a prick" said David.

"Unbelievable." said Steve. "That was so cold. Brrr," Steve mocked Mr. Nash, shuddering and repeating "brrrrr…."

Dave pantomimed holding himself in a blanket shuttering from the cold, his face drawn, his eyes down-cast, and depressed like a concentration camp inmate. "brrr…" he said. Then he threw back his head and laughed it off. "I'm hungry. When do we eat?"

41

"Let's get past the city and stop somewhere in Jersey."

"Let's smoke." said Dave. He loaded a dainty tortoise-shell colored plastic opium/hash pipe, crumbling the hash between his thumb and fingertips. It resembled brown sugar. Dave lit it with a cardboard match, inhaling deeply until his lungs felt near the bursting point and without words offered the seeping pipe to Steve. Dave held the pipe for his friend's convenience. Steve leaned over to toke, still grasping the steering wheel with both hands and finding the pipe's stem with his outstretched lips. Holding deep inhalations until they expelled them with the CO_2 from their purging lungs, coughing and laughing, then breathing profoundly, the boys enjoyed the peaceful quietude, until Steve cranked up the dashboard 8 track, getting off to Junior Walker and the All-Star's "SHOTGUN!"

Smoking, with Dave drumming hard on the dashboard and Steve dancing in his seat, they got onto the Long Island Expressway in Little Neck. Steve kicked down hard on the accelerator and let the automatic downshift make all four cylinders roar in the Peugeot's French accent. The boys set out for Hollywood. They were comedy writers.

Hollywood or Bust:

They took turns driving, making pit-stops, eating fast food, drinking Pepsi and eating "no-doze". They drove afternoon into night through the day and into Kansas City, Missouri. They planned a night in Dave's mother, Naomi's suite at the Hotel Bellerive on East Armour Boulevard. Naomi hadn't stayed in the sanatorium too long (who could blame her), but she did not take her boys back when she recovered (who could forgive her?). She remarried and pursued a career as a gambler. The boys slowed for blinking lights expecting to aid a motorist in distress, but were arrested instead for speeding.

"Do you boys know how fast you were driving?" said a large corn-fed policeman.

"We slowed down for the blinking lights." said Steve.

"You were going sixty-five in a thirty zone. I am going to issue a citation."

The boys exchanged glum glances with each other respecting the officer's authority as he scribbled them a ticket. They were carrying enough contraband to warrant prison sentences and did not want to initiate excessive investigation.

"Don't leave the state before arraignment. That will be August 21st."

"Can we go now?" said Steve, who was doing all the talking and hoping that Dave would not add his mad-cap spin to the situation.

"You can go, but do not leave the state before arraignment."

Later that afternoon, the boys found their destination. The Hotel Bellerive was a fancy place. They were greeted by Tommy, the bell captain.

"Hello, Mr. Samuels. This must be your brother. Hello, Mr. Samuels. We've been expecting you. My name is Tommy. I am here to make your visit comfortable. If you should need anything, do not hesitate to ask me."

The boys looked at each other and at Tommy and did not laugh, which required effort. Tommy was a stout middle-aged man with a black toupee that looked borrowed. He resembled Howard Cosell, but not as handsome. The boys were unwashed and unshaved after driving from

43

Wednesday afternoon through to Friday. They were unkempt. They tried to blend in, but in Kansas City, gentlemen wore ties and jackets while ladies wore dresses and gloves. The boys' hash infused aroma, with luck, might pass for funky adolescent body odor. They were self-conscious and embarrassed. What a terrible first impression they were making. Who were they to even think of laughing at Tommy? He was captain of the bellman and he was every bit of it; freshly shaven, deodorized, perfumed and powdered. He wore spit-shined glossy black cap-toed shoes. Over his white shirt and clip-on black silk bow-tie, he wore a black bellman's uniform with crimson ribbon piping on the slacks, and matching fleur-de-lys epaulettes with braids on his shoulders.

"Mr. Samuels." Tommy called the boys and they did not respond.

"Mr. Samuels." The boys turned around, looked at each other and David responded, trying not to express exasperation.

"Yes, Tommy. What is it?"

"Would you like me to take your luggage to the bungalow for you, now?"

Steve raised his eye brows and hunched his shoulders towards Dave and Dave said. "Yes, please. Thank you, Tommy."

"Thank you, Tommy." said Steve. Tommy led carrying Steve's large brown Samsonite, and Dave's stuffed laundry bag. The boys followed empty handed as middle-aged and slightly stooped Tommy schlepped the luggage, keeping up a cheerful patter, touting the many luxury features of the hotel. "The Café Boulevard serves three meals a day from 6:30AM until last seating 10PM weekdays and 11PM on Saturday and 9PM Sunday. Snack bar is open from 8AM until 5PM with poolside service.

44

Naomi, Dave's mother had married a Mister Joe Samuels, and called ahead to let the hotel staff know that her sons were coming to stay in her bungalow. *Why did she lie about the boys being her sons? She was a compulsive gambler. Was she a compulsive liar too?* Steve thought to himself.

Naomi and Joe were in Puerto Rico starting a credit card company. Dave and Steve played along. "Yes, Tommy, I am David Samuels and this is my brother Steve."

"How long will you boys be staying with us?" said Tommy, who seemed suspicious and amused. The boys were feeling like frauds but it was a convenience to just sign the bills with the make-believe sons' names.

"Not long." said Dave.

"Well, you can order anything you want from the Café Boulevard, which is one of Kansas City's finest restaurants. The snack bar and room service are available from 8AM until midnight. Our hotel staff will make it our business to see that you have a comfortable visit. Maid service is provided to your bungalow every day, with fresh sheets and towels. Be sure to let me know if anything is not to your liking."

Tommy was wearing them out, but they listened intently and hoped that he couldn't tell that they were stoned. Steve considered the possibility that because Dave's mother and her husband were con-artists, that Tommy was suspicious about them too. Dave suspected that Tommy was gay and was hoping that the boys would like him.

The boys found that they had a well decorated duplex suite called "Bungalow A" which opened onto the pool deck. It was attached to the

45

Bungalow B where Mr. Brooks, a widower lived with his teenaged children, Mark and Sue.

Dave called his mother from the bungalow to thank her. She agreed to pay all their bills at the hotel. The boys were instructed to sign everything "Mr. Samuels." Naomi even suggested that they stay all summer in the bungalow because she wouldn't be needing it. *Maybe she really was clairvoyant,* thought Steve, *because how could she know that they couldn't go anywhere until after his court date?*

After she confirmed that both of them could sign for everything, Steve recalled that Naomi had been generous with them before when she married Joe at the Delmonico Hotel in NY. She rented a suite for Dave and all his friends during the reception. The teenagers had a wild pot party with excellent snacks. They sang and danced show tunes. Dave was president of the high school thespian society and many of his guests were actors. Westside Story, Oklahoma and Wizard of Oz were played at high volume as the talented kids danced and sang . Maybe Dave couldn't forgive Naomi for being such a lousy mother, but Steve could; first the Delmonico, and now the Bellerive. Living it up on Naomi's account was OK.

Steve planned to visit the Missouri state employment agency when it opened on Monday. He would need a job in Kansas City if he was going to be there all summer. He had only saved $200 for his aborted trip to Hollywood and Dave had less.

Pretty cool, thought the boys, as they lit up their hash pipe and tested the hi-fi and TV. There was a well-stocked wet-bar in the great room, and a neat little kitchenette which opened across a white marble dining counter

46

with four red patent-leather cushioned barstools. The white leather couch was a sleeper, and upstairs was a master suite, where Dave made himself comfortable. Steve was happy when the couch opened. This accommodation was nicer than either boy was used to. And there were no abusive siblings and parents to turn heaven into hell.

On TV, Dean Martin was having Dom DeLuise substituting for the summer show. They loved Dom and imitated him often. "Sava fo de end!" They said it to each other as a running gag, cracking each other up every time.

Jonathan Winters had a show too. Nobody was funnier in 1968 than Jonathan Winters. The boys loved comedy, watching it, writing it, and playing it. They had written and played comedy routines in high school and made the other kids happy. Steve had an affinity for ending shows on high notes as the curtains were closed because he could not resist pushing entertainment beyond the limits of decency, decorum and good taste.

On one occasion, Steve played Big Bad Billy Joe opposing Dave's character, the old west sheriff. In a showdown at the saloon, the boys started off with verbal joists, like, "OK, Big Bad Billy Joe. If you must know, somebody stole all the GO (general organization) membership cards."

"Oh yeah?

"Yeah."

"So?"

"Sooo…somebody saw you throwing the GO Cards off the Tallahatchie Bridge."

"Yeah?"

"Yeah."

"So…"

"So, there is a stage coach leaving at noon. Be under it."

"Yeah?"

"Yeah."

And then it got physical. BBBJ twisted the sheriff's big nose. The sheriff twisted BBBJ's nipple. BBBJ twisted both of the sheriff's nipples. The sheriff ripped off BBBJ's shirt. It was a prepared tear-off costume shirt. BBBJ ripped off the sheriff's shirt, which was the same type. More purple nurples, flying hats, head-nuggies, and then BBBJ ripped off the sheriff's pants which brought the house down as the sheriff hammed and minced around in his boxers. So the sheriff tore of BBBJ's pants and the boys started wresting on the floor which was an ad lib. That is when the curtain came down. For weeks after the show, kids who otherwise did not know the boys referred to them as Big Bad Billy Joe and The Sheriff.

That is one example, but about enough for now. The boys were comedy writers and comedians. They were ready for Hollywood, with a layover in Kansas City.

The next day they went to the Café Boulevard for breakfast wearing tan chinos and pastel polo shirts, trying to look respectable and to not laugh too much, at the goofy mid-western hicks. David ate sugar pops and drank milk. Steve preferred eggs, bacon, potatoes and toast with orange juice. Dave signed, Mr. Samuels and left a large NY style tip.

Funny:

Later, in the bungalow they smoked hash, and stepped outside to the pool. They swam and read, played shuffle-board and watched as the crowd gathered towards mid-day. They had heard that professional sports teams put their players up there and were not surprised to see the Kansas City Spurs and Kansas City Chiefs with their families. They had heard that American Airlines had a flight attendant school in the hotel, and were pleased to see many pretty young ladies sunning themselves on lounge chairs. To their amazement Ethyl Merman came out to the pool with an entourage. She was staying at the hotel while starring in "Call Me Madam" at the nearby Starlight Theater.

The star-struck boys watched the party of show-people in awe. They tried not to be noticed staring. They played cards, and scrabble, drank Pepsi and ate club sandwiches with potato chips and pickles. After a couple of hours they decided to meet their neighbors.

Ms. Merman was stretched out semi-reclined on a chaise lounge. Tan and busty, her black sequined one-piece bathing suit was more for posing than swimming. It pushed her well-oiled breasts upward and outward. Her hair was a stiff, black bee-hive. On top of that, tilting backwards, perched a pretty, straw sombrero with a pink pastel band. Her sun-glasses were like a Mardi-Gras mask, big, hot-pink glossy plastic with rhinestones glittering on the corners. Her torso was thickened around the middle but still smooth and well-muscled, or was it the stays in her girdle that created a healthy illusion? Her legs were still in good shape and her high-heeled open-toed black slippers had pink feathers shading her perfectly painted red toe nails. She sipped a drink with an umbrella in it. Several chorus boys and girls sat on chairs surrounding close by to her and her co-star, Russell Knight, who was famous for his crest toothpaste commercials in the NY Museum of Natural History. There Mr. Knight wearing a pith-helmet observed the ivory tusks of mastodons. In KC he wore a cabana-set and semi-reclined next to Ms. Merman, frequently giving the back of her hand soothing strokes with manicured finger tips.

Ethyl Merman was holding court, when the boys approached. They were careful not to block the high sun light which shone into the star's face which was moist with lotion and sweat.

"Hello, Mrs. Merman," said David. "Are you staying here at the hotel too?"

Ms. Merman looked at him. He was a good-looking young man and she was moving her nervous lips, smoothing her red lipstick before speaking; holding her curled tongue behind her teeth. She slowly licked a streak of lipstick off her front teeth. Dave continued as it seemed like Ms. Merman was interested in hearing more. "My brother, Steve and I are staying here at the hotel too. My name is Dave. We are staying here in the bungalow." Dave gestured with his right thumb over his shoulder, like a hitchhiker.

"Oh, you're brothers." she said.

She looked at Steve who was wearing a green speedo and aviator sunglasses and then looked back at David who was wearing tan trunks. Dave had large blue eyes under bushy eye-brows. Steve was tall, dark-haired, and light-skinned. Dave was more compact, bronzed and blond. "You don't look like brothers to me."

"We're half-brothers." said Steve.

50

"Well, OK. Have you fellas been out to the Starlight Theater to see our show?"

"Not yet, Ms. Merman, but we have seen you in so many movies. We are thrilled to meet you in person." said Dave.

"Well, you must come out to see our show at the Starlight. We are doing "Call Me Madam" tonight at 8 and every night this week, with an extra show on Sunday at 2PM, lights out on Monday."

"We will be there tonight." said Dave.

"Well, nice to meet you Ms. Merman. I can hardly wait for the show," said Steve.

"OK, boys, it has been nice meeting you. Enjoy the show. See Yas."

The boys went back to their side of the pool and resumed playing games, although they had their hearts in their throats from the experience of meeting a genuine showbiz legend.

The next day, the boys could hardly wait for the entourage to arrive at poolside again. By then they had made friends with Mike the lifeguard and his girlfriend Joanne, who was in the chorus and part of the entourage. It was easier to approach Ms. Merman knowing one of her group. This time the boys were more familiar, having seen the show and already having made friends in the chorus. The show was first class and they praised the star and the rest of the cast profusely. Ms. Merman gestured with her nose toward the bungalow and asked, "How can a couple of young fellows like you afford such a swanky bungalow?"

"Well, we are comedy writers." said Steve.

"Is that so?"

"Oh yes. We write for the Dom DeLuise Show," said Dave.

51

"Do tell," said Ms. Merman.

"Oh, yes and the Smothers Brothers, Dean Martin, and Jonathan Winters." Dave continued, nodding his head, closing his eyes, pursing his lips, feigning a cool and understated confidence.

"Jonathan Winters, huh? I didn't think anybody could write his stuff." Ms. Merman said. "He's kind of crazy." She twirled her index finger near her temple, lifted her sunglasses with the tip of her finger. She looked around at the entourage. "Know what I mean?" She rolled her eyes for everyone and put her glasses back down on her nose with her pinky. "Crazy!" She started laughing and the entourage started laughing. The boys started laughing. She stopped laughing. The entourage stopped laughing. Only the boys were still laughing, so they stopped too.

"Well, he doesn't do it like we write it, but we give him something to work with," said Steve.

Ms. Merman looked at Russell Knight, who had his hand on hers. Then she looked around the entourage who had been hanging onto every word of the exchange. Then she looked at Dave and Steve, and then back to Dave. "Well, tell me, Dave, or is it Steve. I can't remember who is who?"

"Yes, I am Dave."

"I am Steve."

"OK, boys, let me ask you a question." She looked again at Russell Knight and then at her cast, and then back to the boys. "If you write for all these Hollywood shows, then what are you doing hanging around the pool in Kansas City, Missouri?" She made a gesture out of hunching her

52

shoulders and nodding her head and holding out her hands with palms up, as she looked around to her group and back to the boys again.

"Well," said Dave, "we like to get away from all the parties in Hollywood so that we can work. Out here there is less distraction, so we just ride horses, go swimming, play tennis, and when we go inside, we write."

"Good answer, I am sure. That sounds like an awful lot of activity, riding horses and all, playing cowboys and Indians, I imagine."

"Yes. We do play cowboys and Indians," said Steve, wondering if she too was clairvoyant. *How did she know a detail like that?*

Ms. Merman said "How do you manage to find time for writing?"

We write late at night." said Dave.

"I would like to see what you are doing. Do you think that you could grace us with a sneak preview of some of your material?"

"Sure. We would love to. We will be writing something fresh tonight. We can try it out on you tomorrow right here."

"Oh, can't wait!" She chuckled. She looked around her group and they all started chuckling. Joanne was chuckling too, and she winked at the boys when they noticed. They were "in".

That night, after steak dinners at the Café Boulevard, the boys returned to their bungalow. They turned on the TV to the Dom DeLuise Summer Comedy Hour and tape recorded the sketches. They smoked hashish, reenacted the routines and where the recording ended, they stayed in character and continued improvising. Dave's Panasonic reel-to-reel tape recorder caught the act. Then they wrote down the best part and practiced the routine. They amused themselves. They fell down laughing at each other. Dave held Steve's mouth closed to make him stop joking because it was making him hyperventilate. Steve was torturing Dave with take after take, just for fun. They were hilarious, brilliant, inventive, and still unknown outside of their hotel suite, but tomorrow would be their big break, entertaining Ms. Ethyl Merman.

The next morning the boys refined and practiced their comedy routine and smoked more hashish. They fueled themselves with lunch at a poolside table, signing "Mr. Samuels" as had become their habit. They both ate creamy peanut butter and grape jelly sandwiches, with potato chips. Steve drank chocolate milk. Dave had Pepsi. When they saw Ms. Merman and her entourage assembling nearby, Dave let out a loud burp, which Steve found too funny. Dave tried to make him stop laughing and that made Steve laugh even harder. Dave tried putting his hands over Steve's mouth but that just made them both more animated and conspicuous. It did not prevent the entourage from noticing them although it is doubtful that anyone had paid attention to the careless burp.

Dave noticed first that they were being eye-balled by the entourage, so he and Steve straightened out and approached them. "Good afternoon, Ms. Merman." The boys said the same greeting in rapid succession like Eddie Haskell on "Leave It To Beaver" talking to Mrs. Cleaver. Joanne was looking at them and nodding her head back and forth laughing to herself.

"I see that you boys are enjoying yourselves, as usual." said Ms. Merman. She looked around her group chuckling and they all started chuckling too; including Joanne, who winked at the boys. Steve looked up at the lifeguard station and saw Mike, probably asleep behind his dark sun-glasses.

"Oh, yeah, we always have a good time together, whatever we do," said Steve. Dave shot him a sharp look, still annoyed about being embarrassed by his laughing at the burp.

"Yes, wherever we go, we make a point of having some fun," said Steve.

"You boys are great pals, aren't you?" said Mms. Merman.

"That we are," said Dave.

"Well I hope that you boys had a productive night, writing comedy for TV because we can sure use a few laughs."

"We did, we did," said Steve. Dave opened his eyes wider than usual, lowering his chin, raising his bushy eyebrows, and exhaling through his mouth, audibly.

"Would you favor us?" said Ms. Merman.

"Well, said Steve, "this takes place in a psychiatrist's office. The doctor's name is Doctor Jeckyll. The patient is Mr. Hyde."

Dave said, "Dr. Jeckyll, please. You gotta help me."

"What seems to be the problem?"

"I am trying to find myself, but I am lost, hopelessly lost."

"Well, we can try therapy."

"I tried therapy. It doesn't work on me."

"But you have never tried my kind of therapy. I call my therapy 'hide and seek '. You hide and I seek. Sometimes I find."

"What do you find?"

"Yich."

That was a punchline, so Dave looked at Ms. Merman who was laughing slowly, "Ha, ha, ha, ha" she laughed looking right at Dave and then right at Steve. "You boys are funny." She looked around her group and raised her right hand parallel to the pool deck in front of her shoulder and said "funny, ya know what I mean?" She pivoted her flat hand from a limp wrist and looked around the group again "funny". Then she laughed slow and hard and so did her group. Joanne looked at them laughing and winked.

This was the high-point in their budding comedy career. They made Ethyl Merman and her entourage laugh. Then they went back to their table, sat down and played cards, just to settle their nerves.

Hotel Netherlands

The next morning, Steve went to the Missouri Youth Employment office and was placed immediately with a job as "houseman" at the Hotel Netherlands at 39th and Main. He was instructed to report to Mrs. Campbell the next morning at 8am.

Steve was prompt arriving at about 7:45, having given himself an excessive margin for error in finding this new location. Parking his car in the lot behind the hotel, he noticed that several other cars had groups of Negroes in and around them. A gregarious man with a mock-officious air introduced himself as Jarvis. He invited Steve to join the party, explaining that there was a staff meeting before work every morning. Jarvis then asked Steve to contribute to refreshments, suggesting $2. Steve complied at once pulling the dollar bills from his trouser pocket. A slow-eyed skinny woman gave him a 7oz Dixie-cup to hold and poured him some vodka and orange juice, without ice. "Cheers!" said Steve, holding up his cup. Jarvis touched his cup to Steve's and so did the lady who provided the libation. She looked into Steve's eyes but seemed cheerless, offering neither her name nor a smile. They drank without talking and then had another. Jarvis suggested that they might introduce him to everyone, but that it was time for work. Steve fell in with the group as they entered the employees' entrance in the old building's rear, through a screen door that sprung closed, bouncing and rattling after them.

The Netherlands Hotel was a short step up from the flop-houses that Steve had seen during his sojourns to skid-row on the Bowery in NY. Its once grand lobby had a high ceiling and several blown bulbs. It would be Steve's job to dust the ceiling and replace the bulbs, after he mastered the requisite skills. Steve reported down in the basement to a pale skinned, white haired lady named Mrs. Campbell. His co-workers all dispatched to their assignments without coaching. During Steve's interview with Mrs. C, a neat-looking slim white man in clean work clothes and gray hair went in and out twice, picking up assignment papers, casting what seemed like ironic glances and going off to perform technical maintenance.

"Well, Steve. I want you to go up to room #914 to meet Henry Jackson. He is gonna teach you how to clean up an efficiency." Mrs. Campbell picked up the black bakelite house phone, dialed a few numbers and talked to Henry in a calm affectionate southern accent.

"Henry. I'm sending up the new boy for you to train." Her accent was thick but intelligible. This is how it sounded. "Teach him erry thang y'all know 'bout clinen dem efficiencies, an fo gawd's sike, show 'em how to warsh them dirty winduhs. Don't make me tell y'all bout them winduhs

57

again. That's raht. I want them windahs clined tuhdayay. You unnerstain me, naow, doncha, Henry? Tell me you unnerstsand about the winduhs, Henry? Well, OK. Ahm sendin hiem up to see ya raht now. You take good care and show 'em how to do a good job and no dilly-dallying, you heyah?"

"Now lissen heyah Steve. Y'all git on up the elevator thar and find young Henry at room #914 and do whateverall he says. He's a naz baw too, really, I s'pose. Ya just do a good job and we gonna be awraht."

Steve rode the stuffy elevator up, noticing that the hotel was mostly empty except for some Negro chambermaids of varying ages who looked like they might also be cheap prostitutes or former prostitutes who having lost what they had of good looks to advancing age, and hard-living were reduced or elevated to cleaning rooms, depending upon your opinion of those two jobs. He had seen them drinking in the parking lot, but did not yet know any of them. He wondered if these women were too poor to buy clothing that fit which was likely the case, and/or if they preferred to show off their breasts and hips, by stretching the material of their clothes and busting open the buttons and zippers. Whether it was intentional or not, the clothing along with their inebriated loose jointed hip swinging gaits gave the personnel a sleazy look. Steve did not find it objectionable in that way, but it was unexpected and he couldn't help but notice and wonder. They were so foreign to his limited experience. He tried not to stare or catch a woman's eye in a way that might be misinterpreted as flirtatious. He hoped that averting his eyes would not seem hostile, but did not want to give these sad women the wrong kind of encouragement. On the occasions when inebriation allowed him to drop his defense and cop a peak, it was like looking at the topless Africans in National Geographic Magazine and having the pictures look right back at him, some deadpan, some smiling, and some winking.

Room 914 was locked. Steve knocked a few times and there was no response. He wondered if he had mixed up the room number. He tried wiggling the knob, and knocked again. He could hear talking inside. He knocked harder. This time the door opened a crack and he could see a brown eye looking out at him. "You da new baw?" said Henry. His drawling accent was similar to Mrs. Campbell's, but more percussive and gruff.

"I am Steve. Are you Henry?"

"Yeah." He unlocked the door and opened it just enough for Steve to enter sideways. Henry then closed the door with its lock and chain. Steve took this as odd. "OK. It's like this." Henry lowered his gaze towards his crotch and unhooked his belt. He was a tall skinny man, maybe twenty, a little older than Steve. His hair was straightened and shiny black. He had a big pompadour frosted in electric blue. Steve became uncomfortable when Henry plunged his hand deep into the crotch of his pleated trousers but was relieved when he pulled out a flat glass pint bottle of whiskey. Henry fastened his zooty trousers and said, "Come on over heyah." Henry sat down in a greasy old easy chair in front of the TV. Get yosef a chayah and siddown."

Steve pulled a straight-backed, chipped-up, white-painted wooden chair from the kitchenette and sat next to Henry and began watching "As The World Turns". Steve thought that only women watched that show. In fact the only person he ever saw watch it was a housekeeper that his mother hired, and she got fired for watching TV during the day which his mother told his father was lazy and insipid. Henry unscrewed the top of his whiskey bottle and took a slug. He offered it to Steve who took a sip.

"OK," said Henry. It like this heah. We can clean up dis joint in half a day and den Mrs. Campbell, she gonna give us annudah joint to clean, and den annuddah. You get dat?"

"Yeah," Steve started to answer.

"Not yet. Don't talk yet, cus I ain't trew talking to ya. Yuh unnerstan? Don't talk, jes lissen heah." His accent reminded Steve of Red Barber, the sportscaster for the NY Yankees, but a pissed off Red Barber.

Henry took another swig and passed the bottle to Steve who followed his boss's example. Steve had heard his mother tell his father that he was too impressionable.

Henry looked at Steve, leaning his head toward him, sort of peering into his eyes for deeper understanding, it seemed. Then the phone rang. It rang several times. Steve wanted to answer it, because he was prompt by habit, but let it ring, deferring to Henry's experience and judgment. After ten tedious rings, Henry picked up the phone.

"Yeah. He heah. Yeah. I shown him dah oven. It a mess. An da flow need scrapin. The man what lived heah was a pop-drinkin fool. He leave him bottles errywayah a'drippin an a'dryin on de flow, makin it all sticky like sheelack. It gonna be hard scraping it all and cleanin it. I teachin the baw erryting i knows. He OK. I knows. Don't foget da windus. OK. I put em on ta da windus raht now."

Henry hung up the phone and resumed teaching. They shared another drink and another. Steve was more of a hash-head than a boozer and the six or seven drinks that he had downed had taken a toll. He was drunk.

"Well, Stebie Wonder," said Henry. "Mrs. C say y'all got to learn winduh cleanin, so, take off yuh belt and wrap it round yo han." Henry was drunk too.

Steve took off his belt and wrapped it around his left hand and, following instructions from Henry, he looped the buckle onto the long upright handle inside of the casement window.

"Pull dat. Feel dat. OK," said Henry, indicating the tension in the belt.

Steve tested the belt on the casement window. He said, "Solid, Baby!" He was starting to feel "sharp-drunk" and kind of cool.

"Awride!" said Henry. His thick accent was getting more slurred.

Steve sat on the window sill following Henry's instructions. Henry gave him a bottle of generic blue window cleaner and a rag. "Awridee. Now I wash de inside ah de windu and y'all wash de outsahd."

Steve sprayed some cleaner on the window and then wiped it clean. He noticed that Henry was meticulous, slowly getting every spot off his window pane, even using his index finger nail to pick tiny particles of dirt off the glass. Steve followed his example, leaning back, arching out of the ninth floor window with Main Street down below. Steve was afraid of heights, so he did not look down and concentrated on cleaning the outside of the windows. It was going alright until a gust of wind blew the window wide open and unseated him from the narrow ledge. Thank goodness he was tied to the casement handle because he was hanging beneath the window sill with his arm fully extended like a bull riding cowboy when the wind blew the other way, closing the window and pinching his calf. If he wasn't so drunk, he would have been in a panic. He forgot that he was afraid of heights. This was just not the kind of thing that he would ever do except that he was under the influence of alcohol and Henry's tutelage. The wind blew again widening the opening in the window and Steve tried to pull himself up.

"Hey, Henry, give me a pull, here. Take this spray bottle and pull me up." He was getting sober. Henry was holding onto Steve's ankle with one hand and had his other hand inside Steve's waist-band, trying to bring him back in.

"Watch out," screamed Henry in a manic falsetto as the wind nearly pulled him out the window too. He let go of the waistband and Steve pulled himself up with the belt.

"Fuck, Henry. Give me a hand." Henry helped him inside the window.

The phone was ringing. Henry picked it up. "Yeah. We doin da windahs. OK." Henry hung up the phone. "Mrs. Campbell say it time fo lunch."

In the elevator Henry looked at Steve and Steve looked at Henry. They were both shaken by the near disaster. Henry looked right into Steve's eyes and started a slow deep huffing laugh that smelled like whiskey. He was nodding his head "yes" and Steve was nodding his head "no". Jarvis got on the elevator on "4" and rode down to the basement with them.

In the boiler room, lunch had begun. Old Roy had a large tomato can sitting on the boiler. He had been slow cooking hot dogs and boiled eggs since 8AM. His grandson, Little Roy had a large glass jar with several cockroaches trapped inside.

"Little Roy" barked Old Roy. "What fool thang you doin wiff yo cockaroaches now?"

Little Roy was looking at the bugs in the jar, holding it at arm's length and then bringing it up close. He pressed his face against the outside of the jar, like a child looking through a toy-store window at Christmas. He rolled the glass across his face from eye to eye. And then he held it back with his elbows bent for another perspective. Then he responded to his grandfather:

"Ain't no fool thang. Dees damn bugs, they gonna die." Roy threw the jar against a cinder block wall next to the hot water tank and the glass shattered. "Die muddafucka. Did muddafucka! Die muddafucka," said Little Roy as he stood over the shards of glass and scampering roaches. He stamped his feet, crushing his prey and exclaiming with each kill, "die muddafucka!" Little Roy was laughing in contented amusement at the scurrying prey and shaking his head back and forth. It was more the kind of gesture you might expect from an old man playing with his grandchildren in awe of their cuteness and overcome with his own affection for them.

Old Roy said, "Now what I tell ya, Little Roy?"

"Shut up, you ole fool."

"OK. I gonna eat yo hot dog and I gonna eat yo egg. See how you like dat when yo git hungry, an y'all gonna be hungry, and dat ain't no damn lie."

"I don't care, Grampa. You can stick it up you."

63

"Aw raht, aw raht, now Roy," Jarvis interrupted. "dat enough ah dat. Let's be goin outa lunch and get some frahd chicken and show dat new boy, Stevie Wonder around."

With that Jarvis, Henry, Steve, Otis and Little Roy went up the basement steps and out to the parking lot. They all got into Steve's maroon Peugeot and enjoyed his open sunroof. Roy stood up and stuck his head through to feel the breeze. The car lurched onto 39th Street and Little Roy hurt his neck. If Jarvis and Otis didn't stop him Roy would have hurt Stevie Wonder for the sudden move. Oblivious to the threat from the back seat and to any pain he might have caused, Steve was still sharp-drunk. He followed Jarvis's instructions. They stopped at a store and took a collection. Henry ran in and got two six-packs of Colt 45 malt liquor, because they hadn't had enough to drink already and the day was getting hotter. As they finished their beverages they threw the empties out the roof with finesse.

"Wait a minute…ah…slow down here, Stevie Wonder…" Otis said as the car approached an intersection crowded with Negro pedestrians. Otis reached out the window and slapped a sexy looking young woman on the ass, hard.

First she looked around in shock and then she shouted. "Otis, you jive motherfucker."

Otis was a handsome young man, twenty-six and he had charm and confidence which women found irresistible. He also had a sweet nature and great sense of humor which Steve admired. "Oh, Stevie, how was your weekend? I bet you had you some pussy. I had me some pussy too. Oh, Lordy. I had me so much pussy I couldn't come if you called me."

64

Otis shouted to the outraged female who seemed to just be acting outraged and actually pleased with the attention she had received. With all the women on the corner, Otis chose her ass to slap. "Later, Baby. I ain't through with you."

"Is we goin to Colonel Sanders now?" said Roy.

"yah always want to eat chicken," said Henry.

"ain't nuthin wrong wit chicken," said Otis.

"Stevie Wonder. You like fried chicken too? said Jarvis.

"Yeah, I love it."

Soon they were at Colonel Sanders, standing in line drinking. The girl behind the counter was young, pretty and blond. Her uniform looked like a Halloween nurse costume, with a couple buttons open to show off her lacy bra. The boys were pushing Steve to ask her for a date, but he was feeling shy and embarrassed by the attention to his sexual prowess. He nearly lost his temper with Henry, but couldn't help but laugh along with his new pals. When he ordered thighs, Otis started a discourse on white meat and dark meat which Steve felt pushed the boundaries of good taste, even his. The young woman was not flustered and knew these fellows. "OK, Otis, I know how you like your chicken."

"I like my chicken the same ways I like my women."

"How's that?" said the waitress.

"Southern fried," said Otis. The boys all broke up like it was the funniest thing anybody ever said.

"Finger- licken good," said Jarvis and nodded his head, adding to the fun and taking high-fives.

"Yes, yes, yes. I like my chicken like I like my women, finger-licken good," said Jarvis who was pleased with himself.

"Nobody aksed you, fool," said Henry.

"You da fool," said Jarvis and it looked like he might deck Henry, until Otis put his arm around him and said.

"Southern fried is finger-licken good, right Stevie. Y'all like you chicken like you like yo women, Stevie?"

"It's all finger-licken good to me, especially the dark meat." All the boys said "woooohhh!!" And the waitress winked.

Otis said, "sorry sweetheart. Stevie Wonder likes him da dark meat." But I like me some…"

She stopped Otis before he could say another word.

"We all know what y'all like Otis, an yo ain't gettin it here."

"Wooohhh" said the boys and the other people in line were laughing too.

After many changes in the orders, special requests, wisecracks, and complaints from other customers about wasting lunch-hour time, Steve finally got to order the chicken and paid after collecting from his group. They ate chicken while driving and drove further into the neighborhood so that they could visit Roy's wife. Steve couldn't believe that anyone as young and crazy as Roy was married.

"How old are you, Roy?" said Steve.

Roy just grinned.

"I can't believe that you are married already."

Roy grinned some more. He seemed proud to be such an accomplished man and didn't feel that he needed to explain. He wasn't exactly married, but they met his young wife, who looked too young and who had a couple of babies. Roy and the boys gave her their left over coleslaw, potatoes, gravy and biscuits. Roy shared his Colt 45 with her, made out with her and let her lick the chicken grease off his chin; leaning against her while she leaned back against the utility poll. She held her babies out wide, making room for Roy to feel her up and lean against her humping. After a few minutes of entertainment, Jarvis pulled Roy back into the car and the crew returned to work. As they left, Steve noticed that Roy's wife looked happy sharing biscuits and gravy with her babies. It had been a happy little mission. Roy seemed satisfied too. They had done a mitzvah.

The chicken lunch stabilized Steve, but he was way passed tipsy and had passed through "sharp drunk". He was getting tired and wobbly but good enough to fake going back to work. Mrs. Campbell had Jarvis take him to the old abandoned grill on the main floor for some instruction in restoration. The restaurant had a shut-off cursive neon light on the street and a sign with similar logo over double doors off the lobby. "The Netherlands Bar & Grill" might have been a decent place before its fall to dereliction. When it closed it was not cleaned. It had been closed for a long time. Jarvis and Steve pulled open the double doors and found that there were no dishes, pots, pans or kitchen tools, but that the fried food oil was still in the deep-fryers which were built in to the counters. It was thick like jelly and had many large cockroaches preserved in the rancid amber grease. Jarvis surveyed the job and decided to have some sweet wine, a Taylor port of no particular vintage. It had a dark and complex aroma. It was syrupy sweet with aftertastes of rotten fruit and mildew. The worker and his apprentice drank plenty before getting down to the hard work at hand. They worked well together late into the afternoon; sipping and cleaning, telling funny stories, and amusing each other. Steve learned that Jarvis had been a professional boxer, was an expert in all matters of satisfying women, and an enemy of the police, having punched his way into jail on several occasions, never backing down and always maintaining his manly dignity. Jarvis also confirmed Steve's suspicion that the women who worked in the hotel were maids now because they were too old to be prostitutes, but that they could still be had for a low price. Steve also learned that all the other workers had gotten their jobs like he did from the Missouri State employment agency, except that they went to work right after they were released from prison.

When it was time to quit, Steve was rip-roaring drunk. His car seemed like a trusted old horse. He rode it out into traffic and could hardly drive at all. He didn't know how it happened, but he was glad when his friend David appeared and took the wheel. They got back to the Bellerive and walked through the immaculate lobby, but not before Tommy spotted them.

"Why, hello Mr. Samuels." He was talking to Steve, who was oblivious. Dave just wanted to help him back to the bungalow and let him fall asleep.

"We didn't see you today at the pool, Mr. Samuels. Are you alright, Mr. Samuels?" Tommy was taunting David. David was trying to stay cool.

"He's really tired. Today was his first day at work."

"He looks like he worked very hard, today."

"Yes. I am sure that he did."

When the boys got back to the room, there was a party going on. Joanne and Mike were there and several young girls and boys from the Starlight Theatre chorus and American Airlines flight attendant school, in bathing suits, were listening to show music and sipping cocktails. Joanne helped Dave put Steve onto the bed upstairs, where he just passed out, missing the party and dinner.

As it turned out, the cocktail party would become routine as Dave enjoyed the atmosphere of the bungalow and friendship of show people. Steve learned to moderate his drinking at work and the summer settled into something of a routine. It was great having new stars visit the Starlight every two weeks. The boys got to meet Arthur Godfrey, Forrest Tucker, and Al Lewis.

The girls who were training to be flight attendants were of more interest to Steve than Dave and that became a point of contention, as Dave repeatedly discouraged Steve from taking advantage of them in the bungalow. Was he protecting Steve's girlfriend from back home who was touring Israel while they were stuck in Kansas City? Dave got hysterical laughing when Steve got close to girls. His laughter was infectious. While it was great fun, Steve wished that Dave would like one of the girls who always came in pairs and groups and leave him to manage his own personal affairs. What was so funny about Steve unhooking a bra or pulling off a bikini bottom? It made Dave want to have pillow fights and spray soda. These young mid-western girls were easy. They seemed just as happy playing silly games as they were letting Steve relieve them of their excess clothing. Go figure.

Poaching:

When the supply of hashish starting running low, Henry Jackson introduced Steve to Player Jerry, who had a barber shop for Negroes deep in "the neighborhood" as Henry called it. Player Jerry had a business card that said "Player Jerry". It was iridescent satin, blue and green. Jerry had a similar hairdo to Henry's, but his electric-blue frosted pompadour was a bit more subdued. His barber jacket was perfectly fitted and he was smooth in every way. He suggested that Steve come alone to meet him in the alley behind the barber shop at 3AM with as much money as possible, at least $300. Steve agreed to this, because he did not want to get into an argument, but every time Henry reminded him about the deal, Steve had to remind Henry that it wasn't a good deal for him.

Little Roy warmed up to Steve after a while and invited him to go hunting with him, Henry and some of their friends who did not work at the hotel. Their idea of hunting was to get a station wagon and fold down the seats. One of them would drive out into the country, while the others would lie down on their bellies with rifles and shoot out of the rear over the tailgate at farm animals, dear, dogs, mail boxes, and anything else that they could raise their sights on. He wanted to be friendly, but this did not sound like fun.

Steve told Dave, Mike, and Joanne about all the characters he was meeting and all the offers that he was refusing. Mike who was several years older knew some local people too, and he arranged for the boys to join him and Mark who lived next door in Bungalow B and played bass to go poaching pot from some Mexicans who had a secret growing patch.

That night the boys got into a van in the hotel parking lot with a hippy looking guy, except that he looked older than any hippies that they knew. He was pretty old, about thirty-five, and he wasn't the happy hippy type. He had long straight hair and a cowboy hat. His tee-shirt was tie-died and he had pucca beads, but there was something intense about him, and uncool. He made everyone else put on blind folds after they got out of town. It was night and they drove blind for a long time. When they arrived at their destination, the blind-folds were removed and the boys took flash-lights, laundry bags, and serrated steak knives.

They were standing in a grove of marijuana trees that were all about ten feet tall. The boys started bending the plants down and cutting off the top foot or two without discriminating between male and female plants. There was an argument about which were the more potent, but there was no resolution, and the plants' genders were indistinguishable to their untrained eyes. The patch was infested with voracious mosquitoes who feasted on the dopey boys. The insects swarmed and sucked, which made the boys work faster. It was a hellish hot night of confusion, and it ended when all the laundry bags were full of fresh pot.

Back in the van, the boys sat on their sacks of pot, and put on blindfolds again. When they took them off, dawn was breaking and they were speeding down a desolate highway. The creepy night was over and they were going back to Kansas City. As they smoked pot and drank royal crown cola, their moods were lifting. A band of hippies appeared like a mass hallucination. They were hitch-hiking on this desolate road, thrusting their thumbs in manic desperation. These were real hippies; dirty, long-haired, tie-died, innocent youngsters. The van slowed down

71

and took them in. They sat on the sacks with the boys and their partners.
The hippies were grateful to get stoned.

"Wow man. We have been hitching from San Francisco to Detroit and
this country is dry, man, fucking dry," said one hippy.

"Yeah man," said another, "fucking dry."

"Dry as a motherfucker," said the lone Negro hippy who wore a Detroit
Tiger's baseball cap.

"Motherfucking dry," said the lone girl hippy.

"Man this shit is good."

"Yeah, we have some good shit" said Mike, "but not much left."

"Back in San Francisco, we had Acapulco Gold," said one hitcher,
reminiscing.

"Yeah man, we bought a quarter pound for $25," said another,
bragging.

"Man, that wasn't gold. That was good weed but that wasn't gold,"
said his brother.

"It was gold man, Acapulco gold," he said.

"Man we were dealing lids for $15, like it was nothing."

"Hey, we are sure glad to meet you dudes."

"Yeah, man. Thanks. This is some righteous weed."

"Man we haven't had any weed, since Colorado. Fuck that."

The boys listened to the beat hippies complain and smoke for about an
hour before letting them go. The whole time that they were riding,
smoking and rapping about weed, they were sitting on bags full of it.

Back at the hotel, the boys brought their haul into their duplex and
started curing it. It was a load. They took the screens off the windows

72

and scattered the leaves on the screens to dry. They put more inside the oven and put the oven on warm. They put some in pots and pans and roasted it. They tried soaking it in vodka and then drying it, as an experiment. The entire apartment was full of weed and the boys were smoking like demons, testing all the drying techniques and suspecting that their booty was weak. Then the door knocked.

"Maid service."

"Not today, thank you" said Dave. The phone rang. Dave answered it.

Of Mice and Men

"Hi, Joe. Oh. You are. Oh well, OK. You are. Well, do you want me to come and pick you up? Oh. You are. Oh, well it is not really a good time. Oh, you are. No. It is OK. Well, no just me and Steve are here. Yeah. Steve Samuels. Ha. Yeah, right. OK. Sure. We'll see you in half an hour."

Dave had just spoken to his mother's new husband, Joe Samuels. He was in Kansas City and was on his way from the airport. He would be in the apartment in half an hour.

YIKES

The boys scrambled to hide the pot. They gathered it in its various states of refinement and combined it all into a laundry bag and a pillow case both of which Steve carried over to Joanne and Mike's hotel room for safe keeping. Back in the bungalow, Dave cleaned up as best as he could without a vacuum cleaner, picking up crumbs with a butter knife and dabbing hard surfaces with a damp washcloth. He sprayed some Lysol around the apartment and opened the windows for fresh air. It was 100

73

degrees outside, so he closed the windows hoping to avoid suspicion. *Why would anybody want the windows open on a July day in Kansas City when they had air conditioning?*

Steve returned and helped Dave clean up, but they kept finding more pot, in the oven, on top of the refrigerator, in the ice bucket. And then the door opened and Joe Samuels was home at his Kansas City headquarters.

"Hi boys!" said Joe.

"Hi Joe." said Dave. "You might remember Steve from the wedding."

"Steve Samuels." said Joe laughing.

"Hi Joe." said Steve, laughing too, smiling and trying not to seem stoned.

Joe had a small suitcase which he lugged in and put down next to the couch. In his other hand he had a handsome thin attaché case. Joe was short and middle-aged with beady brown eyes and a prominent rounded beak. He wore a high, double-dimple crowned, narrow snap-brimmed straw hat with a snazzy royal blue silk band. He had a pencil thin black mustache, like Bud Abbott's. He was natty with a dull kind of flash. His gray muted plaid tropical suit looked freshly pressed, which was pretty good considering the oppressive Kansas City heat. Joe's black wing-tipped elevator oxfords were highly polished. His powder blue hanky matched his silk tie which had a substantial diamond stud pin set in platinum. He wore the pin high, about six inches above the closure of his three button suit, so that it showed, making the tie billow between it and its half-oxford knot. Joe's collar and cuffs were white, but the rest of his shirt was powder blue. The lapels and cuffs on his shirt all bore his initial "JS" embroidered in a darker blue. His posture was straight but not

74

athletic. He took off his jacket and hung it in the closet, but did not remove his hat. He wore a ribbed wife-beater which showed through the starched light-weight cotton dress shirt. He didn't show any perspiration. He seemed cool and slow. He looked out into the living room and snorted a few quick breaths, opened the closet again; this time taking an even more audible sniff. He looked at Dave and said with a New York accent:

"Mouse terd. I smell mouse terds. Dis place got mice. You seen mice?"

"Mice?" said Dave, dropping his jaw and looking at Steve and then at Joe. "Mice?" He said it again raising his eye-brows.

"Yeah, mice, Goddammit," said Joe. "I'd know that smell anywhere. I come from da Lower Eastside and believe you me I know mouse terd when I smell it."

"Mouse terd?" said Dave.

"Yeah, mouse terd. Definitely mice!" Joe picked up the phone and dialed "O".

"Hello. Tommy. This is Mr. Samuels in the bungalow. Yeah. I just got back and the place has mice. Can you believe it? Yeah. Thanks. She's fine, thanks, but there's mice in here. I can smell 'em. I'd know that smell anywhere. Yeah, I'm sure. This place is definitely got mice, so…don't give me so… so get the exterminator in here at once. You know what I mean? Right now. Yeah. You better believe it. Right, right now. Get that exterminator in here. Don't' waste time. You got it. We're going out now. I'm taking the boys. We are going out to have a nice dinner and see a movie and when we come back, we don't want no mice. You understand me. Tell me what you are going to do as soon as you get off

75

this phone. Yeah? Thank you. Right now, Tommy. You're damn straight."

Joe hung up the phone. "Didn't you boys smell nothing? Christ, it smells like a mouse manure factory in here. This place smells like mouse-terd headquarters. A cat could be very happy and never go hungry hanging round this joint. He could eat mice for breakfast, lunch and dinner and never get hungry. He could invite his friends and have a mouse Thanksgiving dinner. What's the matter with you guys, that you can't smell that terd? Jesus Christ. It stinks from mice. I can't believe that you guys can't smell it. What the hell's wit you guys? Huh?"

Dave looked at Steve and Steve looked at Dave and then Steve looked at Joe and said, "I did see a mouse just last night. It wasn't the first time I saw him either, but I didn't think it would be polite to complain what with my being a guest and you and Naomi being so generous to us and all." Steve then looked at Dave.

Dave looked at Steve and then at Joe and said, "I saw the mouse too. In fact I saw two mice chasing each other around the kitchen, but I didn't want to complain either. In fact I think there might have been more than just two, but they all look the same to me. There could have been lots of mice. I don't know how many exactly, but we did see some mice."

"Yeah. You're damn straight dere's mice. Didn't want to complain? What's a matter with you boys. I pay plenty for dis place and it ain't supposed to have no mice. Dat fucking Tommy. What a nerve. 'Are you sure it is mice that you smell, Mr. Samuels?' Can you believe that?"

"He is an asshole," said Steve.

"He is a schmuck. He doesn't know anything," said Dave.

76

"He is a smendrick, that Tommy. His bow tie has elastic around his neck! For Christ's sake. What kind of cheap lousy bowtie is that? It's a bow tie for spastics who can't tie a tie. That's what kind it is and if he don't get rid da mice today, right fucking now, I'm going to take his tie and pull it out and let it snap back and knock out his fucking adam's apple, da fuck. 'Are you sure that you smelled mice?' What else would I be smelling if wasn't mice? Who's he think he's talking to? You boys have got plenty to learn. Take a deep breath. Smell it. Remember it. That's what mouse terd smells like. Don't ever rent a place that smells like this. I hope that you never have to live with it like I did when I was a kid. Now let's get outa here and let the exterminators do their job."

"Where are we going?" said Dave.

"I am going to buy you boys the best steak dinner in Kansas City while I visit with my dear old friend Manny and then I am taking you to the movies and then we're coming back here to sleep so that I can catch an early flight back to San Juan."

They walked briskly past the pool with Joe carrying his jacket over his shoulder like Frank Sinatra, and the boys wearing wrinkled cotton slacks with polo shirts. Steve followed Joe's directions driving to a steak house called "Carmella's" which was attached to an Italian pork store. They ate dinner at about 4PM. They were the only customers there, but the staff all knew Joe and seemed glad to see him. Manny came down and sat with them. Manny had a drink but didn't eat any of the steaks that Joe ordered insisting that they have the creamed spinach and his favorite steak fries, which were just French fries with the skin still on. Joe insisted that the boys have strawberry short cake, his favorite while he went to another

77

room with Manny. The boys enjoyed their cake with milk and a lady came out with brownies and acted like a doting grandma watching the boys eat and asking them about school. Her name was Rose and she told the boys that she was a friend of Naomi's and that Joe was good to her.

After dinner Joe directed them to an art movie house where they saw "Jules and Jim". The boys giggled a few times during the intimate scenes which seemed to bother Joe. Later back at the bungalow, Joe sniffed in the closet and around the living room like a terrier. "There better not be no more mice. If you boys see a mouse, I gotta to know about it. You hear me. I want to know!"

Joe went upstairs and left the boys downstairs to share Steve's sofa-bed. They smoked hash, watched TV and laughed too loudly. Joe told them to keep it down because he had an early flight out and needed to sleep. The boys were so relieved that mice took their rap that they couldn't help laughing some more.

"Jesus Christ. What is the matter with you boys? You are giggling like a couple of school girls."

That made it even harder not to laugh and the boys were holding their hands over each other's mouths and biting the pillows, trying not to laugh, eventually settling down and going to sleep. In the morning Joe was gone.

DAVID NASH WAS PRESIDENT OF THE THESPIANS.

Dave died when he was thirty-nine from acute renal failure. His feet were swollen to twice normal size. His brother properly described him in his eulogy as "The best and the brightest". Here he is (middle), also pictured left to right, Peter Newhouse, stage manager, Clare Lowell (stand-up comedian), formerly known as Claire Pasternoster, corresponding secretary, Marty Kapell, president. I cropped this picture. My apologies to those omitted. What a fabulous club! Photo credit Ken Siegel

WE ARE IN!

From the high school year book, Steve with Joe Mack and Mark Griffin getting college acceptance letters from State University of New York, where they all had Regents Scholarships to attend New Paltz, New Paltz and Binghamton. Photo credit Ken Siegel, who also died even younger than Dave Nash.

THE EFFECT OF THE PSYCHEDELIC REVOLUTION ON THE INDIVIDUAL IN SOCIETY:

Burt drove Steve and Joe up the New York State Thruway in his Navy Blue Cadillac. Steve sat in front and his friend Joe sat behind him enjoying the red-leather luxury. They listened to Burt's swinging music which the boys preferred to plush silence. Slowing the car and opening the power windows, Burt quieted Peggy Lee and found a shady spot to park.

"Gadzooks! I can smell the pot already." said Burt. "Driving in this lot is enough to get the car stoned."

His nose was right. The breeze from the apple orchard was mixing with the sunny September smoke. Other students were arriving.

Burt opened the trunk and the boys pulled out their suitcases, one each. Joe also pulled out a record player which had its stereo speakers attached, one on each end by long pins with the electric cord wrapped around holding it all together. Steve pulled out his trombone which was in a big gray case, containing a slide trombone, valve attachment, several harmonicas, valve oil and enough hashish and marijuana to last a month.

"Well, son, you have arrived."

"Yeah." said Steve. He had not planned to go to college at all, having learned enough in school by eighth grade. After reading, writing and arithmetic, Steve felt that school's only useful function was social. The war in Vietnam on the other hand made attending college a cool hedge against military conscription and its other unpleasant options including prison, underground draft evasion, and/or expatriation. And the prospect of rooming with Joe had appeal. They were friends.

"Thank you for the ride, Burt. It was generous of you to drive me too," said Joe. His gratitude was genuine. Coming from Belfast, Ireland to Big Egg high school, Joe was a brilliant outsider, superior in English, but with a raw Irish brogue so thick that few had the patience to understand and enjoy his satirical wit. He was a gifted soccer player but did not have experience playing the more popular American games of baseball, basketball, football and tennis. Steve taught him tennis, dance and blues harp.

There was always plenty to eat at Steve's house, and Joe appreciated the acceptance and generosity he found from everyone there. His own family having recently immigrated needed to pull together for their modest life, living over a garage behind their landlord's house. His friends had no idea why he disappeared every day at 6PM. It was to join his parents and siblings who all cleaned office buildings and banks until midnight.

"Don't be a stranger." said Burt as he reached out to shake his son's hand. They shook hands and Joe shook Burt's hand too.

"Thanks, Dad."

"Your Mama and I are proud of you, son. Who'd of ever thought that you would be going to college. Our boy! Try not to get into trouble and remember to go to class. We love you."

"OK, Dad. Bye."

"I better go now, because if I stand in this lot any longer I am going to get stoned."

"Heaven forbid," said Steve. As Burt drove away, the boys could hear Peggy Lee through the sunroof singing "My Baby Don't Care for Clothes".

Steve and Joe lugged their cases into Bouton Hall, also known as "The Zoo", where freshmen boys were lodged. They were roommates. They put down their suitcases and bounced on their sagging twin beds inside room #209. They opened the window, closed the door and smoked hashish.

There was a commotion outside. Sal from Brooklyn was wearing just white jockey shorts and holding a laminated hunting bow with a quiver of arrows strapped on his back. He had set-up a target at the end of the hall and was puncturing it from about thirty yards. It was hazardous for students leaving their rooms and somebody got pissed off when an arrow came too close. It was far down the hall so Joe and Steve let the other students deal with it as they continued settling.

They hooked up the stereo and played it loud with Paul Butterfield Blues Band "Born in Chicago". They unpacked in time to the compelling music. The door knocked and it was the RA (resident assistant). He had been knocking a lot before he got their attention. The boys waved their towels to clear the air, and then Joe answered the door.

"What are you guys doing in here?" asked Wally, the RA, straining his voice through the loud music.

"We are playing music and unpacking," said Joe.

"What is that smell?" said Wally.

"It's incense," said Joe.

"It better be. Why don't you guys come outside to the assembly for orientation? It is starting in ten minutes."

"OK," said Steve. He was relieved that the conversation about the smell was over. New Paltz had the reputation for being one of the best dope schools. That and nearly free tuition was why they were there. Only two hours driving to Manhattan had some appeal too. They did not expect to be hassled for smoking in the dorm. It was almost legal. That was their understanding.

"Who does that RA think he is? said Steve.

"What a lot of nerve," said Joe.

Outside in the quad between the red-brick dorms a few hundred freshmen milled around meeting each other. A similar scene was going on in another quad with just the young women. Outside "The Zoo", a young man with a megaphone was giving instructions but few students paid attention. The sun was low and the boys walked to the mess hall as instructed. The food was institutional, bland and edible. Being high, made it taste better. Boys mixed with girls. Soon the teenaged students were outside again with unstructured time.

A few amplifiers were set up and about fifteen students were playing "At the Hop". Steve got his slide-trombone and joined in the "Doo Wop" fun. It wasn't Steve's favorite music, but it was fun playing in the ad hoc band. For many this was their first time away from home. The mood was exuberant. Steve had a bass voice and took the mike to sing his part. Several boys sang the chorus in tenor "Let's go to the hop." Then it was Steve's turn to sing bass "Oh baby." With his slide trombone, he had fun subbing for the absent baritone sax, adding low register schmears at every opportunity and throwing in a few high register glissandos, like elephants trumpeting, he imagined, to give some extra peak to the excitement.

As darkness fell the boys decided to take a few of their new friends back to their room for a more private party. Girls were not allowed, but Sally and Beverly came along too in defiance. Bruce, from the upper Westside of Manhattan was a tall, skinny, blond-haired, baby-faced hipster. He had skipped a few grades and wasn't even sixteen yet. Big slow Gerard from Harlem looked old and world weary. He had big pores, like craters in his cheeks. His brown skinned Puerto Rican roommate Angel from East Harlem was good looking but also older. They were part of a new recruitment drive to enroll Afro-Americans.

Jim from Rochester was a tightly wound little guy with curly brown hair and small thick framed black glasses. His teeth were little, ground down from a case of nerves. He lit up a joint right in the quad and that made him fast friends with Joe and Steve. Jim brought a few stragglers along and they soon filled room 209. Joe rolled a towel and pushed it onto the door's threshold. Some of their dorm neighbors were welcomed inside too. Steve lit some sandalwood incense to disguise the smell. Jim had plenty of pot and turned everybody on. Albert King was on the stereo wailing "Born under a Bad Sign" when the door started pounding. Joe opened it a crack and saw the RA, Wally outside. He was a nice looking boy, just a sophomore himself. He wore jeans and a New Paltz tee-shirt with converse basketball sneakers which were cool. He had a waxed crew-cut that was about ten years too late. He came from upstate near Fort Ticonderoga and needed the boarding discount from being an RA.

He didn't want any trouble, but he was supposed to keep the boys in line and was the dutiful type.

"Oh Fuck! It's Scum Mouth." Shouted Joe right to the RA's face and slammed the door. The door pounded again. Joe opened it again.

"What are you guys doing?" said Wally. By this time there were about twenty freshmen in the little room, ignoring the intruder.

"We are burning incense. You got a problem with that, Scum Mouth?"

Wally was mortified. He was not street smart or tough. He was just a big kid from a small town. Joe had psyched him out. He just went away and never bothered with room 209 again.

"That's my buddy, Joe." Steve said to Jim. "He always knows just what to say." Jim was impressed and puffed a smoky little laugh.

"You said it." said Jim.

Orientation was a good indication of what the rest of the semester had to offer.

Jim was a pot dealer with connections from Temple U in Philadelphia, to Buffalo U, Harper College, Syracuse, and Boston. He traveled and used room 209 to stash. The boys always had plenty of grass in their luggage right under Joe's bed. They smoked and partied, compliments of Jim. Joe even started his own business from skimming a handful here and there. The boys also kept a bushel basket of fresh picked apples in their room and became the center of their freshman community.

The boys were intellectually curious young men and tried going to classes and reading their assignments. Classes were large and the curriculum was pre-assigned for freshmen. Steve showed up for math and his class was conducted in an auditorium with video monitors playing the teacher's lesson. At the end of the taped lecture, office hours were shown for students with questions. This was discouraging and Steve did not return for lesson number two.

Freshman English was an improvement. For starters the class had only about thirty students. Many more were enrolled, but only about thirty showed up. The teacher was young and pretty. Her name was Mrs. Beard. Steve participated in class discussions and Mrs. Beard encouraged him. She asked him to visit her after class in her office. Steve liked this special attention.

"Oh, Steve, I am so glad that you are here. Please sit. I will be right with you." Steve sat in a wooden chair with arms next to her desk. She made a few red pencil marks on a page and closed a book with a card holding her place. She stuck the pencil in her dark brown hair which she wore up in a knot. The pencil in her hair reminded Steve of a Japanese Geisha wearing chop-sticks. Steve did not know what to say and was relieved that Mrs. Beard picked up the conversation.

"Steve. I hope that you will do me a big favor." She pushed her red polished finger-nails up into her hair propping up her bun, and preening for her young student. She showed him her slim profile and then turned back to face him.

"OK," said Steve, trying not to say anything foolish.

"Well. Some of us teachers, faculty wives and young women from in and around New Paltz are involved with the Huguenot Dance Company. Do you enjoy dance?"

"I do," said Steve.

"Well. You look like you're a good dancer and I think we can use you for our show. Do you think that you could come to our rehearsal? It would be so much fun. Would you like to join us?"

"OK. I guess so."

"Can I try something with you?" said Mrs. Beard. She stood up.

"Sure."

"Please come here and stand in front of me." He got up and stood facing his teacher. "Closer." She said.

He stood close enough to observe that she smelled like coffee and cinnamon.

"Now put your hands on my waist."

Steve complied feeling lustful and wondered if he was out of his league.

"Hold me firmly." He grasped her thin waste, reaching around with his boney long fingers and pressing with their soft tips into small of her back, holding the heels of his hands just above her pelvis. He could feel her breathing in and out.

"Now lift me." He bent his knees and lifted her, extending his arms until his elbows almost straightened. She arched like a swan, dropping her head back, shaking out the pencil and letting her long brown hair fall behind her.

In a low voice she purred "Now take a few slow steps towards the window to my count, one, two, and three."

"Like this, Mrs. Beard?"

"That's very good, Steve. Now let me down slowly as I count some more. One, and two, slower, and slower. Continue walking, smaller steps and three, OK. That was fine." As he lowered his teacher, her flat stomach and pleated skirt pressed across his face. He smelled her musky perfume. She shook her hair and gathered it back up into the bun. He stood watching her, saying nothing; trying not to dispel the magic of the moment.

"Can you meet me here tomorrow at 7PM. We have rehearsal in town and I can drive you both ways."

Steve's nose was full of her perfume. "OK. Tomorrow. Right here at 7." he said.

"Wonderful. I'll bring you tights and you'll need slippers. What size do you wear?"

"Tights and slippers?" said Steve. He had never worn either and it hadn't occurred to him that he would be dressed like a ballet dancer.

"I think we can find you some large tights. Shoe size?" She asked again.

"12 D."

That night he dreamed about continuing his dance with Mrs. Beard. He followed her instructions, carrying her to a bed of wild flowers in a small meadow, by a waterfall near Lake Minnewaska, beneath twinkling stars and moonlight.

The other class he liked was "The Individual in Society". He enjoyed reading Rousseau, Thoreau, Emerson and Locke but found that most of the other students did not bother. Again he was asked to visit the teacher after class in her office.

Mrs. Russell was a large ruddy-faced woman. "You are more advanced than the other students and I don't want you to get bored."

"I read the assignments."

"Yes. And you attend class and participate, which is more than the other students do." She continued. "You might find it more rewarding to develop an independent study program. I would help you with that outside of class. Is there a subject that you would like to study relating to this course?"

Steve thought for only a few seconds and had it. "I would like to study "The Effects of the Psychedelic Revolution on the Individual in Society"

Steve chose his own resource reading:

Doors of Perception by Aldous Huxley

High Priest by Timothy Leary

LSD by Leary and Alpert (later known as Baba Ram Das).

As the weather chilled, the boys read and discussed philosophy, and literature, paying little attention to science and math. Their on-campus party was continuous at night with quiet time for reading, music and dope during days. The boys discovered the natural splendor of the Hudson Valley and Catskills, hiking around Lake Mohonk and Minnewaska State Park, casually wandering around the apple orchards and mountain streams nearby. As the leaves changed from green to red and gold, the political climate ripened too. It was 1968. 500,000 American Soldiers were destroying Vietnam. Richard Nixon was running for President against Hubert Humphrey.

On Election Day Joe suggested to Steve that he try ingesting Hawaiian Woodrose, an organic psychedelic substance similar to LSD. Steve had read all the books in his curriculum and interviewed scores of tripping students. He did not require any coaxing.

"Did you ever take this stuff?" said Steve.

"Oh yeah, it was really nice."

Joe handed Steve a double O capsule full of shaved seeds. Steve looked at it and ate it. He drank some orange soda to wash it down.

They smoked hash and waited. Joe would be Steve's guide, which to Steve meant that he had a friend to do things for him if he was too stoned to do them himself. From all his study he had a good idea about what to expect.

After they got high Steve got nauseous which was not unexpected. He had heard that getting off on Hawaiian Woodrose was a lot like getting off on Peyote, which involved some discomfort. Steve didn't know if he would vomit or defecate, so he went down the hall to a stall and went through some changes. He was experiencing every illness he ever had, all at once. He was in a state of metaphysical distress. He puked and felt better. He washed his face and mouth and returned to his room. The walls were breathing and the music "Big Pink" by the Band was awesome. "Lonesome Susie" brought him to tears. Steve had the urge to go outside. It was fall so Joe convinced him to put on the sheepskin coat that his girlfriend had gotten for him in Israel. He wore it with the shaggy side out. It was white with a large orange dye marker that they used in Israel on the sheep instead of branding. Steve had it fitted as a double breasted coat with large brass rings and leather straps. It made him look like Taras Bulba, the barbarian. It made him feel that way too. Something about wearing skin and smelling lanolin fueled his actor's imagination. He was superman in nature. The cold autumn air was invigorating. He felt powerful as he walked into the dreamy woods. He climbed hills and pulled his way through pliable vegetation as he left the trail. He paused to breath, filling his lungs, expanding his chest until full of life and spirit. Feeling meditative Steve asked Joe to leave him alone. Joe suggested that they stay quiet together, but Steve prevailed and wandered off unassisted. He found a waterfall and let it splash its mist on his face until his cheeks were moist with cold tears of grief and joy. All his life, his love, his loss were experienced at once. As night fell, he looked up at snow-flakes spinning downward landing on his eye-lids like tiny white butterflies, melting and streaming down his face. He walked to a higher elevation following a whistling watery sound. He was sweating in the cold night air, and his exposed skin was hot from exertion. He was mystified by an electric guitar solo. It was like something he had heard before but could not place. As he walked towards it he felt himself dancing in its rhythm. He was standing in front of a frozen water fall. It was a wavy ice sculpture hanging from the steep shiny limestone cliff. Water rushed whistling through it. A cave behind it was an echo chamber. He edged his body around the water fall and perched inside the cave watching the water rushing through the frozen column illuminated by the snowy white night. The sound was like Jimmy Hendrix playing against his own feedback. He was ecstatic, full of the sound spiraling out into snowflake space.

Later Steve walked back to campus and emerged from the woods, pushing back some pine trees and finding the football field. As he walked across the yardage he felt an electric energy buzzing through his bloodstream. It was like the water flowing through the ice, but warming the linings of blood vessels with friction. It had an effervescent quality. It was orgonic energy collecting inside him like a Wilhelm Reich full body orgasm. He was concentrating and transmitting energy. His feet were moving him by an unknown master's remote control as he tripped forward without intention or concern. His experience was elegant, perfect and beyond his comprehension. Overcome with pleasure he collapsed on the grass facing up. The current was increasing and there was a snap. His consciousness was changed. He stood up and had a lovely deep blue rush, then apricot day glow with floating electric blue lights. He kept his balance and felt the snow in his shaggy hair. He shook it and brushed it with his bare hands. He realized that he was on the fifty yard line. It seemed significant but he didn't know what it meant. There was music. His feet took him to a party outdoors to warm in front of a bon fire. Big logs sizzled and snapped, sending sparks up as the snow continued to fall. Joe and Baby-Faced Bruce were smoking a joint and greeted him.

"Wow, man. You look amazing." said Joe.

"You are beautiful, man." said Steve.

Bruce burst out the toke he was holding laughing.

"Do you know who is winning the election?" asked Steve.

"I knew you were thinking about that," said Joe.

"I know what you are thinking," said Steve.

"And I know what you are thinking," said Joe.

"Guess what I'm thinking," said Bruce.

"Oh, yes. Give me a toke," said Steve.

"Oh, man. That is amazing," said Bruce and passed the joint to Steve.

The boys were experiencing extra sensory perception, ESP. They continued smoking the joint, knowing exactly who wanted it and when, until it was just a tiny roach and Bruce ate it.

They did not have to talk, but they knew all. They gravitated to the music. It was an election night rally sponsored by Students for a Democratic Society, SDS. A band was jamming like Canned Heat and Steve went to the microphone and started playing harmonica. Then he sang, improvising the lyrics. He had experience playing and singing but this was better than ever. It was automatic. His notes were dancing with the flames in the roaring bon-fire. He seemed to be channeling the haunting sound of dynamic bending high-notes from Little Walter, his electric harmonica playing idol.

Carlos, the leader took the microphone and started speaking. Steve laid back to catch his breath and listen to every inspiring word.

"Tonight we wait for American voters to decide whether Hubert Humphrey or Richard Nixon will carry on this nation's illegal and immoral war in Vietnam. Who will it be? Who the fuck really cares, anyway?" Steve knew it would be Humphrey by nearly two million votes. He had ESP. Joe knew it too. They wrote down the exact vote for later reference to prove their mental powers.

Carlos continued: "Maybe Humphrey will win. Do you think he will end the war?"

"Hell No." chanted the crowd. Carlos encouraged them joining in from the microphone shaking both fists upward.

"Hell No We Won't Go. Hell No We Won't Go!"

"You are damn straight we won't go. We don't care what you say Mr. Humphrey. And we don't care what you say Nixon. You are both war criminals and we don't have to listen to you."

"Hell No We Won't Go! Hell No We Won't Go!" said the crowd.

"What would happen if they had a war and nobody showed up to fight it?" said Carlos.

"Nothing, absolutely nothing!" said the crowd.

"You're damn straight. Nothing. So we won't go. Our brothers are over in Vietnam right now dying for nothing but an election. Dying for nothing but profits for piggish war machine manufacturers and war profiteers. We are not fighting to liberate the Vietnamese people. That is a big lie. The Viet Cong are fighting to liberate the Vietnamese people from our Fascist puppet dictators. Who wants to go kill the Viet Cong who are fighting to liberate their own country from Imperialist Pigs in American Uniforms? Those boys don't know how messed up they are. They are not heroes. They are fools. They want to do what is right and they trust our so-called leaders to make their choices for them, but they are being disrespected and violated. Our Generals are making killers out of them and they are killing righteous Vietnamese farmers for nothing. We don't have to go. We don't have to suffer the draft. Nixon can win the election and Humphrey can win the election, but they can't win their dirty little war. Nobody can win and we won't help them kill our brothers in Vietnam. Hell No. We Won't Go."

And the crowd erupted again, "Hell No, We Won't Go."

"They got an evil sick thing going on called the draft. You can feel it. Man. It is cold. It is chilling. It is killing. Those fascist pigs are making every young man who gets to eighteen years old take a draft card so that they can take you away and make a killer out of you. You don't have to do it. We can take our draft cards and burn them and show those pigs that we don't have to go."

"Hell No, We Won't Go. Hell No We Won't Go."

Steve, who had been thinking about it for a long time before this high moment, took his draft card out of his pocket and walked up to Carlos at the microphone and said.

"Got a light? I want to burn my draft card." It seemed like the time was right.

Carlos said "Who has a light for this righteous brother who wants to burn his draft card? Many lighters and matches were pushed up with bare hands through the crowd.

"Hey man. You sure you want to do this?" said Carlos.

"Yeah, man. Let's burn it. I don't want it anymore," said Steve.

"What is your name man?" said Carlos.

"Steve."

"Alright, Brother Steve is a righteous dude. He wants to burn his draft card. Anybody else?" Nobody else volunteered.

"OK, Brother Steve you want to burn your draft card, so let's burn it."

Steve took Carlos's lighter and lit the corner of the card. His fingers were shaking. He did not know why. He almost couldn't do it. He hoped that nobody could see him shaking. Was it anger or fear? He turned the paper card in his fingers so that it got completely burned. He watched the yellow and blue flames consume the paper and flicked it away with his thumb and middle finger when it got too hot to hold. The crowd cheered. "Hell No. We Won't Go," while he watched the card smoldering into the wet ground. He stomped on the ashes with his work boots.

"Yay! Alright! OK!" The crowd was stoked and the band started playing "Hey Joe" as the party resumed. The singing was raw. "Hey Joe, where you going with that gun in your hand?"

Carlos took Steve back to his minivan which was parked nearby. Inside they shared a bottle of Hiram Walker peach brandy. "Thanks, man." said Carlos. "If more of us were as brave as you we wouldn't be in Vietnam. That was a very cool thing you did tonight. A lot of people saw what you did and not everyone agrees with you and me about how great it is to burn a draft card. There's dudes in prison for doing what you just did. Do you know that there was probably some pigs out there tonight watching what you did? What are you going to do man?"

"Do? said Steve.

Steve liked the brandy and he felt great about burning the draft card. It was liberating. He had thought about this question before because he knew he couldn't go to Vietnam.

"Well man, I might go to prison like Mohammad Ali, but I don't want to do the time. I might move to Canada or Sweden. I'd like to meet some of those free-loving Swedish blonds, but I don't know if I could learn Swedish."

"Don't worry, man. You wouldn't have to talk," said Carlos and they both laughed.

"Or maybe Mexico. I like it there, especially the beach." said Steve.

"You might go to Mexico because you like the beach. Man, you are a cool dude. I like the beach too. Maybe I'll go to Mexico too and meet you there. But what about if they bust you for burning the draft card? That's what I'm talking about."

"I'll deny it." said Steve.

"Man, you are crazy, you know that? You just burned your draft card in front of hundreds of people. And you're going to deny it. I like you, man. You are a crazy fucking guy. Here have another drink." They drank.

"There's no evidence. I could have burned anything. Is there a law against burning a fake draft card or a copy of a draft card?" said Steve. "I could've been burning my social security card and who would know it?"

"Oh man. You can't burn your social security card either. That's a federal offence. You can't even burn fucking money. That would be defacing federal property too," said Carlos.

"Fuck it. Federal Schmederal." said Steve. "I can deny it. Are you going to testify against me?"

"No man. If you don't want me to, I won't, but are you telling me you burned a copy of your draft card?" said Carlos.

"See what I mean? You were a witness and you don't even know." said Steve.

"You are something else, man. I like you. You should be a lawyer, man. You have a brilliant legal mind," said Carlos. "Did you burn your draft card just now?"

"I did, but who else really knows."

"But what would you do? I mean what are you going to do? What if the pigs catch you? Then what?"

"Well, I wouldn't want to go to prison, or Sweden. Canada is really too cold, and I like the USA. Really, I don't want to move to another country. There is no place I would rather go, but if I had to fight, I would go down to Bolivia and fight with Che for the right cause, for freedom."

"You would go to Bolivia with Brother Che?" said Carlos. "Too late, man. The pigs killed him."

"No, really?"

"Yeah, man. It was a real bummer. The fucking CIA murdered him. They tortured him, messed him up and showed his body off to all the peasants so they could to set an example. It was disgusting. We don't call them pigs for nothing. Motherfucking fascist, shit-eating pigs."

"Well, fuck them. If I had to fight and die, I would rather do it for a real cause, like Che. Shit. I can't believe it."

Steve was beginning to feel perplexed by his situation.

"No man. Hell no. I won't go to Peru or Bolivia either. I mean I am almost a conscientious objector and I am not going to kill anybody. But if I had to I would kill a fascist before I would kill a communist. That's all I'm saying."

Joe came into the van and Carlos said, "Hey man, your friend is a heavy fucking dude."

"Thanks, Carlos. Power the people." said Steve.

"Right on," said Joe.

With Carlos raising his bottle in salute Steve and Joe left the van and reentered the party.

"Man, I am hungry," said Steve.

"I think the student union is open," said Joe. "Let's see what they have to eat."

BEFORE WOODSTOCK

On a rainy day in January 1969 I hitched a ride from Costa Mesa to Long Beach CA in a VW mini-bus with a gang of speed-freaking acid-head hippies. They had left Height-Ashbury "on the lam" from the heaviest California rains in thirty years, finding little sanctuary in the south, as persistent showers kept the outside of the bus clean.

Running near empty, we stopped twice in our sputtering route to panhandle for gasoline and jug-wine money. We bought a gallon of each to "keep on truckin." Wahoo, an Apache runaway girl brought in most of the change. She turned on the charm while we all used the gas station bathroom which took about fifteen minutes. This funky parade in and out of their establishment annoyed the Sinclair Oil attendants who liked Wahoo a bit more than the company she kept.

And who wouldn't like Wahoo? Her long hair hung heavy and wet like black capellini. Her breasts pressed up and out, her hips pushed back, and the wet tie-died tee-shirt that she wore like a mini-dress hugged her tight. After she took a big slug of wine we enjoyed her exuberant yelp, "Wahoo!" She was as happy as a little girl blowing out her birthday candles, winking, smiling, and radiating something like love, or the need for it. After another glorious gulp, she handed me the jug.

"Pass that bottle." shouted the guy riding shotgun.

"Right now!" I said and passed the bottle as requested. He took a swig and so did the driver before they passed the bottle back to Wahoo and me.

"Hey, pass that wine back here. It's our turn, dude." called a voice from behind. I skipped my turn and transferred the mountain burgundy as

100

requested to the three old boys who were playing point-blank slap-jack in the cramped-up space between the back seat and tailgate.

Wahoo was our cheerleader and our den-mother. We were happy to watch her guzzle the lion's share. Our fruit of the vine vanished with just three turns around the bus. "You gotta love Wahoo," said the shotgun and looked me in the eye. I wondered at his comment. *Was it an instruction or prophecy?*

I played my Marine Band "A" harp that I had packed for just such an occasion, sucking and bending a rhythmic blues that I had copied from Sonny Terry. Yahoo danced waving her arms up over her head. The driver shook his shoulder length greasy shag and locked his elbows to keep us moving straight ahead. The guy riding shot-gun was bongo-drumming his hands on the dashboard.

Wahoo remembered the lyrics to "Me and Bobby McGee" and sang in unison with the driver and shot-gun while I played harp.

The slap-jack game was shifting from competitive to vicious with zealous slapping and acid-tongued accusations of misdeals and "jumping the gun".

"Slap-Jack!" said one boy and you could hear a fast smack.

"No. Slap-Jack. I call it." another smack, and another.

"Slap-Jack, you freak. Wait until it is time" Slap. Slap. Slap.

"Slap-Jack."

"No. You have to wait." Slap. Slap. Slap. Slap.

"You're a freak. I quit."

"This game has been a seventy-two hour marathon. They've been playing non-stop since San Jose." said Wahoo.

101

The boys were still playing when we stopped to panhandle in Laguna Beach. These road weary sports were wired and giving off a funky body odor with overtones of ozone. The inside of the bus otherwise smelled from dirty clothes, spilled wine and fermented apple cores. There was a missing ingredient.

Another gallon took us to Long Beach where we visited a grand dilapidated Mediterranean-style villa, near the ocean. About thirty alternative life-style pioneers partied with their babies and pets enjoying the gracious open space on the main floor. Laid-back young Mamas rummaged for misplaced personal items like brushes and tubes of vitamin D ointment as they settled in for the night. Some relaxed on stained and torn overstuffed couches and easy chairs. Their babies were filthy and naked crawling among the untrained puppies' pungent canine mess and vice versa.

When I inquired about "combustibles," Wahoo's eyes lit up and she led me upstairs where the lords of the manor held court with frolicking, sweet-hearted courtesans. A clean-cut, blond-haired young man who looked like a Disney guide shared these digs with a shaggy red-haired and bearded partner who looked to me like Ginger Baker, whom I had recently seen at the Anderson Theater on 2nd Av. in NY drumming with "The Cream."

These young men were drug-thin and naked, lying propped up on elbows and pillows in a Hollywood King-sized waterbed holding court. Their girls were cool and focused without any edge or excitement. I felt awkward amidst these too-cool strangers who seemed totally comfortable being undressed in front of me. Although the vibe was friendly and inviting, neither was anybody asking me to join in the frolics nor did I want it. I was uptight and looked at Wahoo. She shrugged her shoulders, wrinkled her nose and addressed the blond leader.

"He came up with us from the south. He's cool. He wants to cop some grass." When Wahoo raised her eyebrows, winked and left the room, I was the only one left clothed in more than sheets, towels, and/or scarves.

A thin brown-eyed adolescent girl with a purple scarf around her waist put a hand on my shoulder and with her free hand put a damp joint to my lips. She blew some smoke in my face. I liked it and took her cue, inhaling deeply while she looked into my eyes.

"Nice." I said looking at the Disney guide, "Tastes good."

"Yeah, it's nice." He said.

The girl gave me the joint and went back to bed and left me smoking.

"Where you going?" he said.

"Up to Westwood, UCLA."

"You want weight?"

"Is this Acapulco Gold?"

"Fool's-gold maybe. It's Mexican from Oaxaca and its light. You could pass it off as Acapulco Gold, but it wouldn't be righteous."

"It's good."

"Oh yeah."

"Do you have four ounces?"

"Do you have $50?"

"I do."

Ginger Baker got out of bed, pulled on jeans, twisted his torso into a fringed buckskin vest and disappeared.

"The stash is off-site," said Mr. Disney. "Relax. This will take a few minutes."

Large KLH speakers did justice to recent stereo recordings. Featured during my stay were the ecstatic Prokol Harem's ubiquitous "Whiter Shade of Pale" and exuberant Moby Grape's "Hey Grandma". Plush carpet, soft ladies and the smoking joint had made this atmosphere down-right deluxe. Small talk came easy.

Ginger returned as promised. I conducted my manly business with the co-regents and lingered still smoking my complimentary taste as the girls partied. I was invited to return anytime.

After business, the gracious hosts invited me to hang-out, have something to eat and crash downstairs.

My appetite had returned and I noticed an appealing familiar aroma wafting up the stairs…tomatoes and onions…hmmm. I followed my nose to the large country kitchen and found a skinny old man (he must have been fifty), stirring a huge pot with a long wooden spoon. "Smells good!" I said.

The stubble-faced chef gave me a broad smile, revealing several missing teeth, and nodded, like a bobble-head doll. He looked like someone I used to know. *Was it Abie, the former CCNY professor gone rogue, who used to score wine and drive us teenagers around in an old Cadillac? Was it the man who took my friend Sue to the prom and created a minor scandal? I heard that someone dosed his chili with LSD and he was institutionalized. Was this him?* I squinted into his twinkling little brown eyes, searching for recognition. "What is it?"

His smile broadened and his eye-brows arched up towards his receding hair line. The nodding stopped briefly, his lips puckered and pursed with great purpose as he announced the fair with careful enunciation and a whistling lisp:

"Rice-a-Roni, the San Francisco Treat!"

It tasted good, even on a dirty plate with a greasy spoon.

IT'S CHINATOWN:
I FORGOT ABOUT IT.

 You can see me in the middle next to the girl with celery magic wand.
It's my party at Hwa Yuan, 40 East Broadway, my favorite Chinese
Restaurant, with my favorite girlfriend. We all went up to the Apollo to
see James Brown Review and downtown for dinner after. I didn't
remember it at all until my friend, Tom told me about it and showed me
the stills, like forty years later. I still forget it all. I must have OD'd on
MSG. Photo credit: Tom Benedek

PURPLE BARRELS

The apartment house on UCLA's Fraternity Row was pink stucco. Bucky's girlfriend Tara's second story pad had a generous terrace. It overlooked Gayley Avenue's entrance to Bruin Walk, a shady paved pedestrian way connecting the busy street to campus. On a warm Saturday afternoon in February, 1969, Steve and Dave joined Bucky, Tara, and Leslie on the terrace, for a jug of red wine, mellow marijuana and spontaneous music. Bucky played guitar, finger-picking Delta blues, while Steve played his harp. Bucky sang a Dave Von Ronk classic, "Cocaine". His voice was both reedy and breathy which gave his music an intimate confessional tone, something like Chet Baker in lament:

"Come here Momma, come here quick,

This cocaine gonna make me sick,

Cocaine, runnin round my brain."

The younger Steve played his harmonica filling in the rests with rhythmic tonguing and emphatic bent syncopation.

"You take Mary, and I'll take Sue

Upside down's no difference 'twixt the two.

Cocaine…spinnin round my brain"

Bucky sat calmly while Steve stood bobbing up and down, using all his breath wailing and hyperventilating in contrast to Bucky's continuing cool. Lesley and Tara swayed and turned with the music as Dave did a more athletic and angular dance throwing his elbows and hunching his shoulders. The wind treated them all with scents of eucalyptus and jasmine. It was a rare warm day in the cold, rainy winter.

Down on the street, Chuck played recorder, blowing hard up to the balcony and dancing like a drunken sailor on the street. *Was he in Montego Bay or Westwood CA? Did he know? Did he care? Did it matter?* "Come on up." said Bucky. Chuck scrambled in the door to the courtyard under the terrace, for the moment, out of sight.

He entered the terrace still playing the recorder and whirling like a dervish. He wanted to hug everyone and it was a good thing too because he looked wobbly and dizzy from all the spinning. Chuck wore well fitted, faded blue jeans. His tic-dicd tcc-shirt was mostly blue with cut-off sleeves and rough-cut into a boat neck. Puka beads and a leather strapped tiki choked his red neck. Even though it was winter, he was barefooted.

"Chuckie!" said Bucky. He hugged him, letting the guitar hang to his side from its strap.

"Bucky! Wow, man. Hey. OK," said Chuck, who was panting.

"You remember Tara" said Bucky and Chuck hugged Tara.

"Hi Chuck. You have had a lot of sun, haven't you?" said Tara, referring to Chuck's red face.

Bucky said, "He always looks that way. Steve, this is our friend Chuck. He's from Hollywood. Steve is from NY."

Chuck hugged Steve and said. "Solid. NY. OK. Wow. OK." His eyes had heavy lids and his brows were arched. There was something sweet about his eyes and mouth.

Steve said, "Hollywood, OK, solid, Wow." Goofing and teasing, imitating Chuck, who was giggling.

"Hey Chuck." said Bucky, "This is Dave. He is from NY too." And Dave hugged Chuck, while giving Steve a funny look. Steve responded to the look by shrugging his shoulders and imitating Chuck's sweet look, arching his eyebrows and nodding his head.

"Hi Chuck. Glad to meet you," said Dave.

Leslie hugged Chuck and said "Hi Baby. I love your hair."

Chuck had wild, bleached-blond, platinum hair, that stood out from his sunburned face. The hair was wavy and coarse. He looked like he was electrocuted. His face was scarlet and still handsome. He had a swimmer's physique with long arms and broad shoulders. He was a surfer. His eyes were wide open and he laughed a lot. He talked so fast, mostly to Bucky that Steve could only marvel at the intense wrap.

"Chuck. Like what are you on, man?" said Bucky.

Everyone gathered around Chuck as he started holding court. "These are purple barrels." He held up a baggy full of pills. "They are 1000 micrograms each." He reached in and pulled out a single pill. He closed one eye and held the pill between his thumb and index finger close in front of his open eye. Then he held it extending his arm and admired it from arm's length, like an artist using his thumb for perspective. Then he looked at it close up and intent as a jeweler. "This is enough acid for four or five trips, or maybe two." He opened his mouth half way showing his teeth in a goofy smile and nodded his head slowly looking around. Then he turned his hand over and looked down at the pill. "Some people might take the whole thing."

"Really?" said David.

"Oh yeah," said Chuck.

"Like a thousand mikes of acid all at once," said Steve.

"Oh yeah." said Chuck nodding. "Easy. Yeah. Maybe 1001"

"Wow." said Dave.

"Yeah, but I wouldn't take the whole thing the first time you try it. Ugggg…"

"What?" asked Dave.

"Uggg…a…uggg…ah, ah…"

Dave and Steve looked at Chuck and each other and then Chuck.

"Are you OK?" Steve asked Chuck.

"Ugg..ah.. You should just take some and then if you like it take some more and make it last longer."

"How long would a trip last?" said Leslie, who had not yet experienced LSD.

"Oh, I don't know. It could last all day." said Chuck.

"It could last anywhere from all day to the rest of your life," said Dave with a wise-ass attitude. Everybody laughed, especially Chuck, who thought it was extra funny.

"Oh yeah, really. Wow."

"Does it depend on how much you take?" Leslie asked Chuck.

"Well…you have to take enough to get off on or it really doesn't work at all. I mean, if you take too little, it might just make you up-tight and waste the hit. But when you take enough you know it because, well, you just know it. It is like 'wow', you know what I mean? It's like "wow".

"Wow." said Steve. He looked at Dave who was laughing. Bucky was shaking his head smiling, like he might go "tsk, tsk" but he did not.

"Are you tripping now?" said Leslie.

"Oh wowowowo…yes, yes, yes. I am tripping nownownow, most definitely, my deardeardeardear."

Chuck was goofing around like an echo chamber.

"How much did you take?" said Dave.

"How the fuck would I know, know, know, know? said Chuck. He was being a wise-ass now.

"Would two hundred mikes really be enough for a first trip?" asked Leslie.

"Like about that much would do it for most people. But if you take more I don't know if it gets you higher or if it lasts longer. It seems like either you are tripping or you are not. I don't know if you trip higher on more or longer on more. You just trip out.

"Leslie. Have you ever tripped?" said Tara.

"No, but I am thinking it might be fun." said Leslie.

"Have you ever tripped?" Leslie asked Tara.

"Yes. I tripped on mescaline, but not on LSD. LSD seems a little edgier to me. The mescaline seemed more mellow."

"Chuck, you are smoking pot, drinking wine and tripping on LSD. Do they go together well? Aren't you afraid of getting sick?" Leslie asked.

"LSD and pot go together like peanut butter and jelly, and wine is like the milk. Are you kidding me?" Leslie looked at Tara and Tara gave Leslie a joint.

Chuck started playing the recorder. Bucky and Steve joined in on their instruments. Tara took a toke from Leslie. Dave started doing a nutty dance that made Leslie crack up and the party continued.

Steve and Dave tried two hundred fifty micrograms each. They swallowed the jagged broken pills with some red wine and waited. After a while Steve felt restless and invigorated and not quite himself. He needed some alone time. He went down to the street to take his motorcycle for a ride. It was parked on the steep slope, right across from the terrace. It was a red and chrome Honda 160, which top-ended at 70MPH. Steve pressed the ignition button with his right thumb, twisted the accelerator hand grip and revved up to the amusement of his friends who observed him from above. Then he popped a wheelie from a standing start and fell right over backwards. He found that hilarious, but had enough sense to park the bike and not go for a ride, just yet. His friends were all glad that he was not hurt and they also laughed hard at the crazy stunt. He came back upstairs and let Leslie sooth his scuffed up hand and elbow. She stung him with peroxide and then blew cool little kisses on his hot spots. "All better," she said. It was exquisite. She had been trying to get Steve into her kitchen and into her bed ever since they met. She was sympathetic to his plight as a draft resister, and found his fearless, outlaw aspect to be romantic. He liked her, but not as a girlfriend. She was too motherly.

The party carried on into evening. Chuck, Dave and Steve dropped more acid to keep the peak into the night. Before Chuck left, Dave and Steve bought fifty purple barrels.

"Imagine if we could always be this high." said Dave.

"Why not?" said Steve, like Dayton Allen used to say it on the old Steve Allen Show.

"And Whyyyyy Not?" Dave said it too.

They cracked each other up saying "why not" over and over, but it was even funnier when Tara slipped between them, put her hands on their shoulders, and said it in a low voice. "And why not?"

They tripped all night. Steve had the keys to an apartment that he had rented near the beach. They weren't supposed to move in until the next day, but decided to go there anyway. They took more acid and went to the Santa Monica Public Beach with Steve driving the Honda and Dave holding onto his waist. They morphed into the motorcycle, and it seemed perfectly natural. They became one well-oiled machine riding in perfect mechanical buzzing bliss, cutting through Santa Monica Boulevard's foggy dawn. Near their new apartment on Frazer Avenue they ditched the bike and walked to the Santa Monica Peer by Muscle Beach. They trucked on the sand like Crumb comic book characters. They had extra power in their steps. They were getting off on an already high trip. They had rockets in their feet strutting high like "Elastic-man", until they found a comfortable place to sit. They played in the sand hallucinating that each grain was a precious, light-splitting electrifying gem. The boys dug deep into mother earth soon reaching the water table. They were dazzled by the infinite diffractions multiplied by the countless ancient marine particles. Pulling their heads out from shallow watery holes, they looked at each other's sandy faces. It was awesome. They became pre-historic and pre-verbal. "You have to come up for air occasionally." said Dave, finding a few words.

All Steve could say in reply was "hhhhhh, hhhhh, hhhh," making a huffing breathy sound without words.

Surfing USA:

They shed their outer clothes and walked into the water. They swam out beyond the breakers, feeling reborn and at one with nature. They saw seals and ORK, ORK they morphed into seals. They swam. They bobbed. They dove and exploded up through the brine. They saw seagulls and they morphed into seagulls. They floated buoyant in the salty swells. The primordial mist was intoxicating. The cool water and warming sun made their bodies electric. Body-surfing they became flying fish with white water crashing over their tails, propelling them with arched backs and outstretched arms. Crashing to the shore they became drift-wood, knocking and rolling in exhaustion with the ebb and flow of the tide. They went back out and body-surfed back in. They went out again, and again beyond the breakers, catching up to the best waves. The boys drifted and became separated. Dave was the stronger swimmer, and he had gone farther out. As Steve was tiring, he noticed that he had sticky globs in his hair and on his body. *Was it an hallucination?* He didn't like it. He had never had a bummer or bad trip and this seemed like a bum trip kind of thing. He looked for David who was far away. Steve tried to call, but a wave hit him and he swallowed water. He tried to compose himself, but the surf seemed to be picking up pace and intensity. He forgot which way was out and which way was the shore. He spotted David again and tried to make a loud taxi whistle, but he could not. There was more of the thick glop sticking to him and he was feeling heavy and afraid of drowning. Another wave knocked him under so hard that he didn't know which way was up and which way was down. He popped up out of breath only to be slammed again by another wave. He couldn't find his friend and couldn't swim towards the shore hard enough to overcome the current which was taking him farther out. More of the gloppy goop was sticking to him, making him feel heavy? Steve swam to the white caps and managed to catch a wave which flushed him to the hard sandy shore. First he just felt the beach with his cheek and realized that he was safe. Then Dave washed in after and crashed just a few feet from him. He had a shocked look in his eyes. They crawled like ship-wrecked survivors. Then they revived as sea-creatures and evolved to amphibians. They crawled on the cool wet beach bedazzled by shimmering reflections and day glow colors, astounded by the filigreed art work in the receding tidal foam. Returning to the warmer sand they were young men again; tripped out with expanded consciousness. They were awed by nature and grateful to be healthy and alive, well...alive.

Dave was more religious than his atheist friend. "I was lifted from the sea by the hand of God. It was the fickle finger of fate that saved us for a greater good. Did you feel that too?"

"I don't know." said Steve.

"This is real."

"It's a trip," said Steve.

"But it's real."

"It's like a movie."

"Really?"

"You know what I mean. We are tripping."

"Then what is that black stuff in your hair?"

Steve had forgotten about the glop and felt it again. Looking at Dave he said, "You have it on you too." And the boys started noticing it was stuck to them in globs the size of ping pong balls. It was stuck in their hair and on their arms and legs. They tried to wipe it off, but it stuck. It was stiff tar. They had gotten tar on their feet at the beach before, but this was a lot of tar. They were confused and were having trouble discerning the trip from reality. They resisted believing anything negative and tried to be positive, but the tar would not come off. They were in their own separate upset frames of mind struggling with the tar and their inability to grasp the reality of the situation. They looked at each other wordless, seeing electric auras that were transformed into twisted wavy rainbow colored god-heads gone haywire. They had experienced beautiful auras before as great pleasure and inspiration without the confusion, but these were perplexed god-heads. They were vexed and could not speak. They needed to talk but each syllable and utterance would be new and unique. As they reinvented language, they would seem to be talking in tongues, saying one thing that meant many things. When they found words, they were profound.

"W, w, w, wow" said David.

"F, f, f, far-f, f, f, fucking out" said Steve

"What did I tell you?"

"What?"

"Oh, man. Let's not talk."

They lied down on the sand, next to each other trying to get warm from the overcast morning sun. It wasn't enough so they chilled and shivered. They could just hear themselves breathing and feel their hearts beating. Blood coursing through their veins felt like flat seltzer. It was still early and no one was near them on the beach. It was off-season, so no lifeguards yet. The boys suffered some mild hypothermia and felt wired from their LSD binge as they recovered from the exhausting near-death encounter with the ocean. Two surfers appeared wearing protective wetsuits to keep them warm. Steve and Dave looked at each other some more and their skin looked blue and purple which they thought was another hallucination. Much later they would learn that they had been tarred by the remains of a disastrous oil-spill off Santa Barbara. It would be an exaggeration to say that it was the environmental shot heard round the world and of course they hadn't heard it, but it turned out that they were caught unaware in a big deal. They figured it out later when they remembered that they saw it on the TV news. Water-fowl looked much slicker, but by the time the oil reached them it had been treated with coagulants and had become sticky tar-balls.

"You are blue, David. What color am I?"

"You are purple."

The boys inspected their hands and looked themselves over, amazed at the cold and oily colors. Again they fell back onto the sand and it warmed them. They fell to sleep and woke up hungry. They wandered off the beach and saw an old arthritic man with gnarly swollen joints, sitting in a wheel chair next to a building wall. He was trying to get warm from the hazy sunshine too. "Hello." said Dave rediscovering his tongue. The old man had a pained look and nodded his head in a negative way.

"See ya." said Steve.

The boys walked to their new apartment at 129 Fraser and walked in. It was furnished and the boys went right to the shower and turned on the hot water. Together they warmed up and pulled off their tarred clothing. They tried scrubbing the tar off using the bar of soap that they found by the sink. It wouldn't come off. They scrubbed each other using wash cloths and soap but it had the effect of smearing more than removing. But they were warmed.

The next sensation was hunger. They put on the sandy outer clothes for warmth and to cover the tar. They took a short walk to Ralph's Market, feeling like freaks, alienated from the strangers that they encountered. Feeling paranoid, they tried not to look at the cashier and imagined that he was looking at them. They knew that they did not look normal. They needed to eat and did not want to get busted. It hadn't even occurred to them that this was their first day in their new neighborhood and that they were making first impressions. They were too tired and weak for trucking. Staggering was more their speed.

Nobody else had been for a swim. Their hair was still matted with tar and they looked like they had just escaped from a desert island, or a mental institution. They felt like Japanese soldiers returning from a remote atoll who did not yet know that WWII had ended. How strange they felt reentering society? It was so weird in Ralph's Market with its rows of merchandise and refrigerated packaged foods. They eyed the Wonder Bread which built strong bodies in eight ways. Peter Pan Peanut Butter, Marshmallow Fluff, Baloney, Oscar Meyer Wieners and Tropicana Orange Juice. They were bombarded by random associations and impulses and tried hard to remember why they were in the store. They bought Carnation Chocolate Instant Breakfast and Milk, believing that they would get all the vitamins and nutrients they needed from a single delicious malted beverage. They paid with wrinkled money. It was as though they had never traded before and the concept of money to barter made strange sense to them. The cashier gave them cups and straws. Out in the parking

118

lot, they sat on the curb to mix their meals. They could hardly swallow the thick and lumpy blend. They had to try several times gagging, spitting and laughing more out of embarrassment than amusement. They struggled just to get the right amount in their mouths and find a comfortable pace for swallowing. What to do with their tongues was a fresh mystery. They were relearning their most basic skills. David burped but they were too tired to crack up. Dave gave Steve a mean look that he had never seen on his friend before. "Don't look at me," said Dave. They continued the meal in chilly silence.

Greg, The Love-Man Stone:

Breakfast made them feel stronger. Steve remembered the motor-cycle. They wandered around looking for it. A faded blue VW bug approached them on the Venice Speedway and they looked inside to see a suntanned young man with long brown hair looking out at them. His car had the scent of watermelon incense burning on the dash-board. Beads and fringes hung from the roof-liner inside and the boys were curious.

"Hey. Do you guys know of some place where I can crash?" asked their new acquaintance referring to a sleeping accommodation.

The boys looked closer.

"Hey, Dudes. Where are you going?"

"We are looking for our bike." said Steve.

"It is around here somewhere, but we can't find it," said Dave with a twisted frown.

"Maybe I can help you," said the man. "Get in. My name is Greg, Greg, The Love-Man Stone."

The boys got in and introduced themselves. They found their bike and with Dave riding on the back and Greg following, Steve drove home to Westwood, keeping the pace slow in the right lane to avoid excessive wind chill. It was a cool winter day and they were shirtless under their light jackets. The instant breakfast had not fully restored their vigor.

Greg helped them move their stuff from Dave's apartment to their new place in Santa Monica. Greg moved into Dave's bed on Gaily Avenue as the rent was paid up for another day.

The boys didn't know it, but the purple barrels that they bought from Chuck had been laced with speed. The LSD was wonderful, but the speed made them want to keep taking more. The result was a binge and a crash. The crash was unlike anything they had ever experienced. It was like being manic-depressive. They were so high and then so low. They tried smoking pot, but it was small relief for what ailed them. This is how lots of recreational drug users got hooked on harder drugs. The despair of the crash was miserable and pot was inadequate to relieve their jangled nerves. Dave and Steve eventually slept it off feeling cold and alone with frozen bones and crawling skin. After this experience they smoked pot harder. The crash subsided and they got back to normal, but they still hadn't figured out that their LSD was laced with speed. They never saw Chuck again. They heard that he moved to Australia.

The Love-Man came to visit, slept over and was hard to shake. He was a bongo-banging beatnik poet who had a compulsion to perform. He couldn't stop and no amount of complaining could cool his enthusiasm for his own art. He had only one piece to perform. It was about Little Red

120

Riding Hood. He riffed on the bongos to accompany himself. He chanted:

"He was cool and groovy. She was young and innocent, but warm and moist. He was cool and groovy. She was young and innocent, but warm and moist. My, what big eyes you have. The better to see you with my dear. He was cool and groovy..."

It was tedious and obnoxious, boring and prurient, incessant and inconsiderate. And the Love-Man had love problems with his ex-wife and his son from whom he was estranged and separated with a restraining order. So the Love-Man made long pleading phone calls to Torrance where his ex-wife tortured him by loving another man who was assuming his roles as lover and father.

But Greg did work. He was a tennis-pro. Among his clients was Peggy Lipton, star of "Mod Squad". She was his main client and he did occasionally pony up some phone money.

Before the ocean ordeal, Steve had grown weary of being on the lam from the draft board. He was tired of spending every day figuring out where he would sleep, resisting Leslie and others of both genders who found his need attractive. He was underground and could not do anything that would bring his whereabouts to the attention of the draft board. The apartment he found was month to month with no lease required. He loved it in Santa Monica near the beach and rented it for $165 per month. He and Dave had a two bedroom pad with eat-in kitchen. The terrace had an ocean view when you leaned far over the rail. The landlord said that Edward G. Robinson used to own it before it was carved up into apartments. There was a call-girl named Carla who lived behind them with her pimp, Tim. Upstairs was a fat lady named Nancy who drank lots of wine and had many men visiting her. She was the jolly type, like Mama Cass.

Steve had found employment as a landscaper with daily income sufficient for rent and motorcycle payments. He sometimes partnered with Bucky who borrowed Tara's car and drove him to auditions. He went expecting to meet Alfred Hitchcock, Otto Preminger or Joseph E. Levine, thinking he would be discovered and groomed to be a realistic cowboy star. He was given job applications that included landscaping the studio grounds. At real auditions which were also known as cattle calls, the other actors were much better prepared, with professional photos and resumes. They were so good looking and well dressed. Where did they get the money required to prepare like that? Were they all sponsored by parents? Were they independently wealthy? To prepare for his big break, Steve binge-read cowboy books and western stories with a particular liking for a biography of John Wesley Harding about whom Bob Dylan would devote an album. He also read Dave's homework from UCLA and helped with assignments, especially ancient history. With all that, he still had spare time for LSD binges which he believed would help him beat the draft by reason of insanity. That is what he was thinking.

Dave continued his studies at UCLA where he was distinguishing himself in Theatre Arts. He was a gifted actor, playwright and poet. He had exceptional memory skills and a prodigious knowledge of ancient history, battles in particular. He even knew Bible, chapter and verse. When tripping, Dave, whose birthday was Dec. 25th channeled Jesus. This proclivity might have helped him too to avoid the draft if the necessity

122

ever presented itself. Any psychiatrist who valued his professional standing would diagnose his prophecy as delusion, and David knew it. He also believed that if Jesus were to come to Santa Monica he would be put into a mental institution with all the other Jesus's, Napoleans, Oedipus's, Hamlets, and assorted other unsettled souls and time travelers.

Miss Vicki:

One day Steve drove Dave to rehearse a movie directed by a graduate student named Joe Casey. Joe was older than the other students. He was an ex-marine who had a grant to direct film at UCLA and his project was about a young GI who cracks under the strain of basic training. Dave was the star and Steve was recruited to hold lights and help out. The climax was when the GI freaked out, screaming "This is my rifle, this is my gun. This is for killing. This is for fun." He said it over and over again with his anxiety and rage boiling over in close-up. At the screening, Joe sat in the audience wearing a blanket and just a jock-strap underneath. He was a large man, with athletic physique, long hair and black beard, like Jesus. At the climax he ran up in front of the screen with the projection shining on him. He threw off the blanket and stood there in his jock screaming the same lines. "This is my rifle, this is my gun." This is for killing. This is for fun." And then it was over. The audience went wild. Joe won an award.

He was great fun to work with and he had cool friends. One of them had the crew over to his beach house in Malibu, for a cast party. They all dropped acid and had a bon-fire on the sand. It was mellow. Steve took a swim. He stood on a rock watching a seagull on next rock. The bird was silhouetted against a big apricot liquid sun. Steve morphed into a seagull, feeling his feet and toes like talons, gripping and balancing lightly upon muscle shells which were cushioned by sea-anemones. The bird flew out to sea and Steve lost his balance, sliding on his back, head first, down the rock's slimy soft surface and splashing into the still, cool deep water. He came up for air surrounded by the salmon colored sunset reflected on the rippling water all around him. A gorgeous mermaid turned into a woman on the shore and he remembered that it was just a trip. He looked again and she was bathing like a Monet painting. He swam closer and she was gone. He saw her again near the bon-fire. She was looking at him, but when he got closer, she disappeared in the shadows. He joined the party and smoked hash.

After the party Joe drove the boys back to Frazer Avenue and persuaded them to let a dancer named Vicki crash with them. She was that girl on the beach. She was more curvaceous than other dancers, with long, damp, wavy black hair, and a prominent nose that suited her classic Grecian face. She was not a kid anymore and had been in Hollywood for several years, struggling for a career. She didn't like the Hollywood halfway house for down-and-out starlets where she had been staying. When Steve and Dave brought her back to Santa Monica, she made herself at home.

She raised a few eyebrows sunbathing nude on the front porch behind low bushes but nobody complained. She enjoyed using sheets and towels as costumes for after shower dance performances. She didn't have any clothes except for the jeans and sweatshirt that she was wearing that night when she arrived. Her bra and panties often hung to dry on the shower curtain rod, giving the cozy apartment a woman's touch. Her overnight bag was small and she borrowed Steve's tee-shirts, which she wore like mini-dresses. She enjoyed frequent, therapeutic long, hot baths to the limit of their hot water heater's capacity.

Her dances were her passion and the boys joined her. The towels were turbans and sheets were togas prompting time-warped entrancing dances into ancient mythical Greece and Biblical Egypt. She danced Arabesque while Dave and Steve did sideways Egyptian struts. Their studies in ancient history included "Oedipus and Akhenaton" by Immanuel Velikovski, which mixed well with "Moses and Monotheism" by Sigmund Freud. They gave a new twist to the story of Exodus, from the Egyptian point of view.

Dave thought his legs were too fat and was obsessed with Oedipus and Akhenaton who also had swollen legs. Was it just a coincidence that the myth of Oedipus and the history of Akhenaton were the same? Oedipus and Akhenaton both called their capitols Thebes, and they both loved their mothers, too much. No coincidence there, or was it?

The theories were jumping off points for fantasies with the boys improvising historical characters and events. They conjectured that Akhenaton, the heretic was Pharaoh during Exodus and that his father was gay. The heretic's marriage to his own mother, Queen Tiye was the historical basis for the Oedipus myth. Moses was a stuttering black Egyptian who gave the Pharaoh fits. When sex charged the atmosphere as in Oedipus with his mother, Vicki seemed to flash-back to a trauma and withdraw. The boys avoided her emotional hot-spots and learned to switch gears into comedy.

She loved gay humor but in the spring of 1969 being gay was Dave's worst fear and Steve's funny bone. They enjoyed acting gay, but just for laughs, like Jonathan Winters and Dom DeLuise. Sometimes Steve had to stop Dave from being physical. "Hey, cut that out, man," said Steve. "Just kidding, man," said Dave. Vicky loved it.

Vicky was in her glory as the one-woman Greek chorus and chorus girl. She danced the great female parts, Queen Tiye, Nerfertiti, and Jocasta. Dave played Amenhotep III (the fairy pharaoh) and Oedipus. Steve played assorted Generals, Priests, and slaves. The boys tested their comedy routines on friends and neighbors but Vicki had stage-fright, so Dave played the females and Steve played the heroes. They received encouragement, especially from gays and blacks and started feeling like the next big comedy thing, like the new Martin and Lewis or Abbot and Costello. Dave was so funny and Steve was the straight man.

When Steve came home and found Vicki wet from bathing, pink and lying on his bed with just a damp towel, he just left her alone out of respect for her extreme vulnerability. She kept returning to his bed with its south facing window and low slanting sun. She slipped into his bed and slept next to him and he didn't even know she was there. When he discovered her snuggled up with him, he couldn't tell if it was real or a dream. There were quiet mornings after crazy nights when he woke up next to her and wondered what had happened and concluded it was nothing. Quiet afternoons were like that too. He never knew when she would come and go. She seemed contented to be alone and the boys were usually active away from home. They liked her, except that she ate their food and did not clean up. She was kind of a bum and they were hustling to keep the party going.

More than once she left the burners on the stove lit and candles burning in the bathroom. They did not lock the door but she didn't even close it when she left. The boys felt that they could not leave her home alone anymore. Steve tried talking to her. "Vicki. You left the stove on. That is dangerous." She seemed shocked and scared by the accusation. "Please. If you use the stove, remember to turn it off." She withdrew. It became uncomfortable and they told Joe. He gave them money and thanked the boys for taking care of her. "Vicki. You got my bed wet. It is OK to use it, but dry yourself off with the towels not the sheets. Is that too much to ask?"

"OK! I'm sorry." She said and cried so hard that Steve was sorry he mentioned it. She cried hard as she looked right at him with an expression that he could not understand. It was so dark around her eyes that he could not recognize her, and she smelled like sulfur and ozone. He tried to hug her, but she ran away into the living room and cried alone curled up on the stuffed chair. She was inconsolable.

Steve drove Vicki on the motorcycle to the half-way house in Hollywood where she used to stay as last resort. She hugged his waist and pressed her cheek to his back. He felt her heart beating, and her deep breathing. That was the closest that they had ever been. He was sad leaving her knowing that she would rather live with him and Dave. He felt caddish, cold, and resigned, like he did when he left his girlfriend in NY. Then too, he reasoned it was for her own good. He could feel her sobbing as they rode up Sunset Boulevard. She knew where they were going.

When they arrived, she got off the bike, looked at Steve with wet eyes, and tear-streaked face. She didn't say good-by and before he could say it, Vicki turned around and went into her old place clutching her little overnight bag, close to her chest.

The Strangler:

After an all-day into all-night LSD binge, Dave remembered that he had rehearsal on campus, so Steve drove him there on the Honda. When they arrived at the theater the young woman who was directing a play called "The Strangler" as her final MFA thesis was having a passionate discussion with the stage manager.

"What's wrong?" said Dave.

"It's Brad. He isn't coming this morning."

"What, again?" said Dave.

"I am afraid we can't rely on him, but there is just a week left for rehearsal. Where can we get another actor?"

Dave looked at Steve who was still sitting on the motorcycle. Steve looked back at Dave. Dave looked at Sandy, the director. She looked at Steve and then at Dave. "Can he act?" she said to Dave. He nodded his head, yes. She looked at Steve. "Would you like to be in our play?" Steve looked at Dave who nodded yes.

Steve said to Sandy. "What would I do?"

"You would play a disruptive stage hand. You won't have many lines to learn, but we need you on stage for every scene and you must show up for rehearsals."

"Disruptive?"

"Yes. We will need you to be able to break Dave's character. Do you think you can do it?"

Dave answered. "He can do it. Just say yes."

"OK," said Steve.

The rehearsals were fun. Steve and Dave enjoyed hanging out and being on stage together again. When the show came, Steve had rehearsed putting a chair on the stage for Dave who was playing a cranky old man. Dave tapped his cane here and there to make the stage hand move the chair from place to place and acted like a needy pain in the ass preparing for his big monologue. In the key scene the stage hand comes back in the middle of the old man's monologue with a police whistle on a lanyard. This is where he would break the character. He had rehearsed it before. He puts the lanyard over the old man's head and it hangs around his neck. Then he says. "If you need anything, just whistle." But for the real performance, the old man had a white wig and fake beard. When the stage hand put the lanyard over his head, he dislocated the wig and beard. Disrupting the character was in the script but this was not. It got a big laugh, in a serious play and was much more disruption than the director had planned. It was almost predictable; Steve on stage and schpielkas for the director. But Dave was the star and rose to the occasion. Steve helped him get his wig and beard back on while the audience laughed. None of this was scripted as the old man ad-libbed and the stage-hand talked back. Then Dave got back into character and really rocked the house, nailing the final moment. It was theater magic. Although it had been written many years ago, it had only been produced once, in 1937 at the University of Michigan in Ann Arbor. Nobody had ever seen it and nobody knew that

129

the script had an extra scene. When it was over everyone was satisfied. "The Strangler" won awards for its director and its star.

Dave was still a freshman at UCLA and I was a non-matriculated draft resister. We were sharing the apartment near the beach in Santa Monica and ran out of hash. When Dave got ripped-off by a bogus dealer on the Sunset Strip we returned seeking restitution.

"That's him! I gave him the money for an ounce of grass and he disappeared."

"You just gave him the money?"

"Well, OK. Don't tell me. I know. I'm a schmuck."

"I was thinking schlemazel."

"And the schmuck who stole my money?

"A schlemiel."

"When did you get so Jewish?"

"You don't have to be a Jew. You know what Shakespeare had to say about situations like this."

"What?"

"Neither a schlemiel nor a schlimazel be."

"Oh shut up!"

"You shut, up. You're the schlemazel who gave him $20."

"Well, look…the schlemiel's walking away. Let's get him and give him a taste of Yiddish law. Hurry up."

I turned the red Honda 160 motorcycle around on a dime using my feet to keep it upright and sped towards the crowd at Dino's, 77 Sunset Strip. There were rich boys in mod clothes and sexy girls in mini-skirts, stylish Afro lads with puffy pirate sleeves and Jimi Hendrix headbands all mixed into the predominant group of buzzed looking youngsters from the Valley making the scene to score. The cops swept the area clearing loiterers every ten minutes. A hustler had to work fast. "He sees me. I'll get him." said Dave.

He jumped off the bike and grabbed the skeevy scammer by the scruff of his neck. I idled near the cut in the driveway. Dave had his throat and the guy was barking in his face. Dave released his grip and the schlemiel reached into his hip-hugger pocket handing Dave a baggy with pills, before getting shoved off with a push in the chest.

Dave got back on the bike. "He gave me five hits of acid, yellow barrels. He says they are a thousand mikes each."

"Great. You wanna drop one?"

"Maybe not."

Tom Marinara came over in the morning. He was a quiet boy from Dave's acting class. He dressed like a Kennedy; khaki pants, blue oxford shirt, wavy black hair over the collar. He drove us to the Palm Springs Pop Festival in his grandmother's champagne Chevy Caprice. All three of us sat in the front seat with Dave in the middle. We smoked Tom's grass and listened to his eight-track, pounding on the dash board while Janis Joplin wailed and cried "Just a Little Bit Harder".

Driving through Palm Springs the traffic slowed. Stores had signs that said "No shirts, no shoes; no service." Old people were wearing cardigan sweaters, because the temperature was only 90 degrees. They frowned and cops gave us the evil eye, so we proceeded, breaking laws with more discretion.

Near Tahquitz Canyon, where the original "Planet of the Apes" was filmed, traffic was crawling, so we ditched the car and joined the pedestrian parade. Brazen young ladies wore bikinis. Others wore cut-off short-shorts and went braless beneath tie-died tees and tanks. Sunshine supermen went shirtless enjoying the benefits of free vitamin "D". Goat-skinned flasks were circulating too and we got dosed with electric wine. This was Easter 1969, before Woodstock and before Altamont. We were enchanted.

Five thousand tickets were sold which was two thousand too many. We didn't know about the event until that morning and didn't care about the music; even less the tickets. We went just to see Palm Springs.

Following the crowd we dallied at an oasis with tall palms beside a bleached craggy cliff. Snow-capped San Bernardino peaks sent melted glittering blue rivulets splashing into a cold plunge pool. We drank it like rain and jumped in to chill. The contrast of hot sun and cold water made us giddy. It was heaven. We climbed up, got hot and jumped in again. We clawed even higher up the cliff and perched to watch talented divers perform. We had the best seats and held up our fingers like Olympic judges, rating mostly eights and nines. Some disoriented climbers mistook us for mountaintop mystics. They wanted to know the secret of life. "Be cool." Was it the electric wine or contact high? We didn't know, but gee…we felt good.

Two freckled and frail looking orange haired brothers scaled the cliff. The elder dove and hit his head on a rock, making a bloody mess. I scampered down and wrapped his cracked scull in my Ghost Motorcycle tee-shirt. The boys staggered out of the canyon like wounded veterans, the younger supporting his traumatized elder.

I wandered through a Hell's Angels encampment which was actually a psychedelic bazaar. There was a tent with some topless girls dancing next to it. A couple of menacing looking bikers stood next to a sign. It said, "Free love, $20/10 minutes." I sold all the acid I had and even traded for some hashish. Tom and Dave stayed back and watched. The Angels tolerated me. We were all outlaws. "Are you insane?" asked David.

"What?" I replied.

"You just walked onto the Angels' turf and stole their business," said Tom. "You can't do that."

"Angels? Where?"

"Just act normal." urged Dave.

"Normal?" I said.

"Shut up." said Dave. Tom nodded suppressing a laugh. "Et tu, Tommy?" said Dave in a sarcastic stage whisper.

At sunset the desert turned cold. Few were prepared with warm clothing. The drive-in theater that was housing the festival was conveniently surrounded with wooden fencing. The future leaders of America tore it all down lighting the desert with scores of bon-fires, liberating the festival for all comers. We clustered dancing like flames, to heathen rock and roll provided by County Joe and the Fish, Credence Clearwater Revival, and Paul Butterfield Blues Band. Later we warmed our feet on the radiant sand walking closer to the stage. At another camp we witnessed a nervous naked teenage girl surrounded by raucous young men. They were clapping their hands in a manner that we recognized as disrespectful and menacing. We pretended to have found Tom's little sister and took her under our protective custody. I gave her my warm sweatshirt which she wore like a mini-dress.

Lee Michaels Group was playing a hit song "You Know What I Mean", which made an impression. Our little sister, Andrea used it as a suffix for everything she said. "I'm hungry. You know what I mean?" "Do you guys have any speed? You know what I mean?" "Are you taking me home? Know what I mean?"

So we answered her that way too. "No speed. Speed kills. You know what I mean?" Might take you home in the morning if you tell us where you live. Know what I mean." "Hey, we know what you mean, so you don't have to keep saying know what I mean. Know what I mean?"

After midnight it was too cold for comfort without my shirts. We noticed cops moving through the crowd in groups, showing a combination of disdain and restraint. We continued our uninhibited revelry, but the vibe was ominous and we were hungry. At 3AM we found Tom's car and started driving back to Santa Monica.

At 4AM I borrowed Dave's jacket so we could go into the diner near Riverside. We were eating pancakes and eggs, treating Andrea to butterscotch Sunday when Lee Michaels Group came staggering past our booth. Frosty the drummer was a big pink dude with a huge platinum Afro. He gave us the peace sign and went with his trio to a distant booth. They were weary. A TV behind the counter reported live that festival attendance was estimated at seventy thousand. We all watched the Palm Springs Police Force moving through the crowd, using their night-sticks to prod the youngsters and cracking their heads open when they resisted. We

135

were glad to be soaking up syrup and not getting our heads busted but I couldn't help thinking about the bloody orange-haired boy leaning on his little brother.

HOLLYWOOD INTERNATIONAL COLOR STUDIOS

In the early spring of 1969, Steve responded to a classified ad in the LA Times for a "photo adv crew". Thinking that it was a job working for a photographer, like the guy who changed film for David Hemmings in "Blow-up", Steve hitchhiked to 6675 Sunset Boulevard, in Hollywood. There he found an office building called "The CrossRoads Studios", where models and pornographers worked. Opening the studio door marked Hollywood International Color Studios, he saw the walls covered with a profusion of eight by ten glossies. They all had one theme; women spreading their labium. The photographer had a fetish.

"Hi. How are you?" said Harry, a plump man of thirty-six with a Howard Cosell toupee.

"I am here about the job offer in the LA Times."

"Direct selling."

"No. Photo adv crew."

"Door-to-door sales."

"No. I am interested in the photo adv job."

"It is door-to door sales, direct selling. You go door-to-door in advance of a photographer who takes pictures of housewives and their babies."

"That is not what I want to do."

"Why not? What else you got to do today?"

"Look. I didn't come here to work as a door-to-door salesman. I am going back to the beach."

"OK. Hey. A good looking young stud like you can probably get lots of girls at the beach. Boy I wish I was young again. You know what I mean? When I was young, when I laid down, the girls mounted up faster than the cavalry. Know what I mean?" Harry pumped his fist and winked hard. He put his left hand up to his lips like a bugle and "Toot, toot, too toot." He played charge. "Hey, I got an idea. How about every girl you bring back here that lets me take her picture naked, I give you ten bucks?"

"No thank you, Harry."

"If she lets me shoot her and gives me a hummer, I'll give you twenty."

"No thanks." Steve opened the door to leave.

"Hey. Don't leave now. How much money you got in your pocket?"

"Eight bucks."

"Why don't you try selling? I got a crew going out in a little while. It's easy. Maybe you can go home with twenty or thirty dollars. How would you like that? What you got to lose? Come on. Try it."

"What would I do?"

"It's easy. Look we have a scientifically formulated questionnaire that is guaranteed to work. Here it is." Harry hands Steve a script. "OK. Now read it to me like I'm a pretty housewife. I know that it's a stretch, but use your imagination. Ring my bell."

"Ding Dong." says Steve.

"Hello" says Harry in falsetto.

"Ma'am, this is a TV marketing research survey and they would like to know your favorite channel is on TV."

"Oh. I like channel 3."

"Channel 3. That is good. Can I ask you another question?"

"OK"

"Ma'am, do you prefer name brands or store brands when you shop?"

"Oh I prefer name brands."

"That is good. Do you have any of the following brands in your home right now, Brillo, Colgate, Wheaties?"

"Oh. I have Wheaties."

"Can you give me the box top from Wheaties?"

"Here it is."

"Mrs. Jones (Harry), you are a winner! Hollywood International Color Studios in conjunction with Channel 3 and Wheaties is awarding you a beautiful 5X7 full color portrait like the one you see here" (Show a picture of a baby.) A picture like this would ordinarily cost you thirty dollars. But you get it free. That is right, Mrs. Jones, Hollywood International Color Studios will have Frank Williams, one of Hollywood's top fashion photographers come right here to your home and photograph you and/or your family for free, because you are a winner. OK, Harry, what is the catch?"

"There is no catch. You are great at this. You are a natural. You are going to make a lot of money selling. All you do is make the appointment and then take a two dollar refundable deposit just to make sure that the broad is there when Frank shows up."

Steve agreed to wait for the crew and go out selling. After a while, the crew had not arrived, but Harry's father Jack did. "Hi, Dad. Steve, meet Jack. He's my father. Dad, this is Steve, our new salesman."

"Hi, Harry."

"Hello."

"Pop. Why not take Steve down to the café and buy him a cup of coffee while you wait for Frank and Tom?"

"OK." says Jack.

"OK." Says Steve, but I don't drink coffee.

"So? You like milkshakes?" says Harry. They got great milkshakes down there." Steve nods yes. "So Pop, buy the kid a milkshake and check out all the sexy models while you wait."

Jack and Steve go downstairs to the café which is bustling with sleazy young women. A dignified black waitress with a great build and well-tailored uniform brings menus. "What can I bring you fellows?"

"What's your name, Sweetheart?" says Jack.

"I'm Suzette. Would you like coffee?"

"Coffee is good. I like it black, like you, but you're so sweet, I could go for some of your sugar on the side. It might change my luck. You must be an actress, or a model? Am I right?"

"Coffee black, and you young man, what can I bring you?"

"He likes milkshakes. Can you give it to him black and white? I know you're an actress because of the way you take a line." She ignores Jack.

"I do like black and white, but I prefer double chocolate ice cream and skip the syrup. Can you put a raw egg in it?"

"Black coffee and chocolate milk-shake, double chocolate ice-cream with a raw egg and no syrup."

"My son, Harry is a glamour photographer. He owns Hollywood International Color Studios. How would you like me to arrange a professional portfolio session for you?" She ignores Harry and goes to counter and then serves them without ceremony. The men sit at a table drinking coffee and milkshake. Jack is in his seventies, an English Jew with clipped British accent, like Terry Thomas. He is dressed in a black and white hound's tooth tropical suit, with white silk tie and straw fedora.

"You should drink coffee. It's good for selling."

"I am stimulated enough. Believe me."

"Look at the bum on that one." says Jack leering.

"Nice." says Steve as he sucks hard through a plastic straw."

"Look at the cans on her." says Jack.

"Nice." says Steve with no problem understanding the British jargon.

"You saw the pictures up in the office?"

"I'm afraid so."

"My son Harry took them all."

"You must be proud."

"He is using a huge new lens to shoot a series of hooded clits in extreme close-up. Did you see those clitorises blown up to 8x10 glossy head-shots. They all look like Dopey and Sleepy to me, but Harry has done the entire series. He calls it 'Seven Dwarfs'. It's his opus."

"He must be a genius."

"You know he plays accordion too. He has a band that plays Bar Mitzvahs and weddings on weekends. That's his main business. Photography is just his hobby."

"You don't say."

"That's where he meets his models. Most of them are Jewish."

"That's funny. They don't look Jewish." Steve sucks hard on the straw and it makes a load noise.

Jack takes a sip of coffee and smacks his lips. "Nowadays, with women's lib and free love, the young girls all want to show off. They got no inhibitions! It's a wonderful country. God bless America! How's that milkshake?"

"It's good. Do you think the sales-manager is coming today? It is almost eleven."

"Don't worry. Frank usually arrives around now. He's probably getting a blow-job."

"Great."

"Oh here he is now. Hey Frank, where were you, getting a blow-job?"

"Yeah, that's right I was getting a blow-job from your daughter- in-law, Elaine. She says that Harry's too tired to give her any because he's always working, so I did her a favor. She says she's tired of his little 'Vienna Sausage', so I gave her a big mouthful of old Frank. Hey who's the kid?"

"Hi Frank. I'm Steve. I understand that we can make some money selling today."

"Making money would be good. Where's Tommy?"

"He's probably getting a blow-job." says Jack.

"He's probably giving one if I know Tommy." says Frank. "Pretty Boy's so cute, he can give me one too. Oh, here he comes now."

"Hi Frank. Hi Jack. Who's the kid?" says Tom.

"I'm Steve. I am the new salesman."

"And I'm the crew-chief so let's stop scratching our nuts and make some bread."

Frank is a big man in his fifties with plenty of long greasy gun-metal gray hair, brushed back into fenders, with a thin pompadour, that hangs over his eye brows. His suit is too tight and overdue for a visit to the dry cleaner. His puffy face used to be handsome and now he needs some bridge work.

142

Tom is pretty. He wears his wavy red hair combed back with a pert DA. His face would be movie-star handsome except for a series of scars; evidence of a tragic car crash before the advent of seat-belts and safety-glass windshields. He is wearing a powder blue blazer, black slacks, and a sheer white shirt open enough to display a golden cross on his smooth pink chest. He holds a clip-board.

The salesmen size up the new kid as they go outside into clammy smog. They get into a red Corvair, with Frank behind the wheel, Tom riding shotgun, and Steve scrunched in the backseat. They smoke cigarettes and banter as Frank drives them to a residential area called Crenshaw District. When they find some hula-hoops and tricycles on the sidewalk Frank stops and lets Tom off. "OK, Pretty Boy. This is your block. See if you can keep your pecker dry long enough to sell some baby pictures. It's almost noon. I'll meet you on this corner at 2PM for lunch. Now, you got your coupons so get your ass out there and make me some money. If you can't make some money, at least get your pecker wet and tell me all about it."

"Screw you, Frank." says Tom.

"Up yours, Pretty- Boy. OK, Kid. Let's get you on a block. How many coupons you got?"

"Ten" says Steve.

"Ten? You got ten coupons? You gonna make ten sales this afternoon? That, I gotta see. Here. Look at that beach ball and the little bicycle. This is a good block. Go on out there and see if you can get some sales or get yourself laid trying." I'll meet you on this corner at 2:05."

"OK. Up yours, Frank." says Steve.

143

"What the hell did you say to Big Frank Otis?"

"Up yours, Frank."

"OK. You're learning fast, Stevie Wonder. Screw you. I'll see you on the corner. Let's see you sell ten coupons. Up mine? Ha. Not today. I gotta headache."

Steve had a great day, selling out of coupons using Harry's pitch. He had twenty dollars in his pocket from deposits plus the eight bucks he started with that morning, and commission due in thirty days. For lunch they went to the Hollywood Bar on Hollywood Boulevard. It offered a free business man's buffet.

"Hey, Hot-shot, how about lending old Frankie Boy five dollars so he can get his other suit out of the cleaners?"

"OK." says Steve slapping five singles into Frank's open palm.

"Could you make it ten?"

"Screw you."

"You're welcome."

"Gin!" says Frank to the bartender." (An aside to Steve) "Liquid marijuana (To the bartender) Keep it neat. Make it a double."

Tom drank martinis with cocktail onions and stuffed olives, licking his fingers after each one. They ate little rubber Swedish meatballs in congealed brown gravy with such enthusiasm that Steve thought they might taste good. He bit one and it was disgusting. He spit it into a cocktail napkin, wiped his tongue and refreshed his mouth with a generic fountain cola. Enjoying his drink and accepting the companionship of his fellow professionals he realized with satisfaction that he had a marketable skill and would always be able to make a living.

CRAZYLEGS AND COSMIC STEVE

The Dance:

At Student Center rock concerts our cosmic tribe pow-wowed. We had our own community spirit dance parties, up front and near the stage. We were a little bit more than just good friends and we were there for more than a little fun. We were there to light up and motivate our less stimulated fellow students. We were there for the visiting musicians, to help them get off! Hello Chuck Berry! Long live Country Joe and the Fish! All Hail Credence Clearwater Revival! Go get 'um Jesse Colin Young and the Youngbloods! We are with you Young Rascals! Welcome to our planet Wilson Picket! Chambers Brothers, we agree completely with Brother Lester, "Time Has Come Today!" And to the Isley Brothers, we concur "It's Our Thing Too!" We were there to dance!

Within our corps were a couple of Jesus-of-Nazareth look-alikes. The rebellious and iconoclastic Jewish bad-boy Jesus was admired most by those among us who had Catholic school upbringings. The "Naz" was ideal, and played well with Buddhist leanings that were getting heavier among our impressionable minds in a free-loving, go-with-the-flow life-style. We liked the physical look of Jesus. It was close to our fashion; drug thin and thoroughly-fucked. And some appreciated the fun-fat smiling Buddha body. We liked the non-attachment of Buddha which complimented our free-love philosophy. We assimilated Alexander Dumas's credo for the Three Musketeers who vowed "All for one and one for all, just like the Beatles who explained it musically with these lyrics "I am you and you are me and we are all together, come together, right now…"

Our raving Jesus Christ in his aspect as Robin Hood, and his frizzy-haired, petit, and flower-powered girl-friend, Maid Miriam played our hip young Dad and Mom. Our other Jesus look-alike and Robin Hood's best man, Brother Alan was a more ethereal Jesus. He often wore flowing white buccaneer sleeved shirts opened to the waist, revealing a golden cross on his lightly haired smooth muscled chest. He carried about him an aura that earned him the nickname, The Prince of Peace. He was irresistible to both genders, omnivorous and promiscuous enough to earn another moniker, Host of Crabs.

Our stable of stars included Lily Lovely (AKA Bad Girl). Bad Girl was 6'3" with smooth, soft olive skin. Her eyes were light green. Her hair was straight chestnut and hung to her ass cleavage like a Polynesian. She was sensuous and dreamy. Amy (AKA Jailbait) liked to say, "I am only sixteen". She was cute and spunky, eager to throw off her clothes, show off all her brand new feminine charms and fuck like a goddess. Her soft-spoken, flute playing boyfriend, Pooky accepted her as an equal ignoring the slight difference in age even if arcane laws might consider it grounds for prosecution. We had a Puerto Rican guy who wandered in and made friends with us. His name was Jesus. He wore a leather pilot's cap with open strap like Rocky the Flying Squirrel. He was great fun and we liked knowing that everywhere we went and everything we did, we did with Jesus; the real Jesus. Include June Flowers, who was an African dancer from nearby Westbury. Her compact body was suitable for Joffrey Ballet where she found a home after leaving us, and then she toured the world

146

taking off her clothes in "Hair". I was a new kid from Hollywood. They called me, Cosmic Steve. I passed myself off as the model for Joy of Loving II. The clean-shaven demonstrator of "variations" was my double. People kept telling me, "You look like somebody." and one thing often lead to another, and another. Our most visible member was CrazyLegs, (AKA Swami Boogaloo). He was tall and skinny, shaggy and bowl-legged, incredibly flexible and rhythmic in every aspect of his movement and speech. When we were all together, the party had arrived!

We enjoyed grassy lawns on sunny days. Lying on our backs in star formation, temples to temples we imagined June Taylor and Busby Berkeley production numbers. In unstructured leg lifts and foot turns we framed the sky with our feet. To combine our energy and get it centered we did eight count rhythmic breathing. We chanted "OHM" for that universal vibration that spiraled through our conch shell shaped inner ears ringing out into the cosmos and beyond the "Waygonisphere". OHM" watching the billowing cumulous clouds prancing like Lipizzaner Stallions or on still days, "OHM" projecting Shirley Temple dancing with Beau Jangles Robinson on big flat screened stratus clouds singing about Animal Crackers in her soup. "OHM" we were awed by stars shooting, and meteors showering at night, wowing as their streaking day-glowed after-images floated in the dark, dissolving in gem-struck luminous dust like fading Roman candle-lit fire trails and disappearing ash in unlit sky. "OHM" and we greeted each other the next day singing like Roy Rogers and Dale Evans "Happy trails to you, until we meet again…" And meet again we did and often, celebrating life's cosmic glory, our energy peaking at first rate rock concerts on Long Island University's Post campus. Our troupe's numbers multiplied in the charismatic rebellion and excitement of 1969-72.

Swami Boogaloo:

It was definitely the peak when CrazyLegs signaled us with his signature dance move, the Swami Boogaloo. It was a difficult contortion for anybody else, but it was effortless for him. CLegs as his intimates called him was 6'4" and skinny, with shoulder length wavy black hair, naturally parted and falling from the middle, often covering most of his head until he dramatically threw it back to reveal his expressive face. Suitable for modeling a Jewish Hippie Icon mask he sported a prominent beak, Elliot Gould lips, and an Adam's apple as big as an early fall McCoun. CLegs had big dark wide-opened eyes that sometimes expanded into sanpaku, like Rasputin's in the old black and white movie "Inside Dr. Caligari's Cabinet", as Rasputin opened his eyes wide to hypnotize and dominate the vulnerable and damned Somnambulist. CLegs's eyes became white pools floating his corneas while his uni-brow arched highly ironic. He dropped his jaw sinking his cheeks in wonder at his own magnificence as he was demonstrating for all to behold. CLegs became "Swami Boogaloo". Bending his knees shoulder width and slightly bowl-legged, with his palms outward and fingertips spread, hyper-extended, and reaching far, far out, he sent his long thin arms upward and backward in a yogic stretch. He reached way, way, way back, bending into a full backbend and extending his hands, easily and rhythmically with slight boogaloo twists, left, left, right, left, right, right, left, right, left, left arching his back all the way, way back and grasping his own ankles to complete the bent-back circle. His profile was a big upper case "Q" and CrazyLegs was serenely pulsating, humping up in time to the music.…Swami Boogaloo rides again!

Once this signature pose was completed, Swami Boogaloo would calmly release his hands from his ankles and spread his fingertips into the floor, shaping them like elephant ears beside his gentle brows on the ground so that he could press his pelvis up and up, rhythmically humping upward with increased vigor to the great above with love. During this penultimate moment of yogic bliss we would hoist a sacrificial virgin (or reasonable facsimile), Amy, Miriam, June or some other feather-weight lovely female of honor to mount our great Swami. We would behold what seemed like the god's making love as Swami Boogaloo's consort would ride him like a camel with one hand on her hip and with her free hand, swirling the imaginary lasso, a la Chubby Checker! Hail CrazyLegs and OHM to Swami Boogaloo!!

Peter Pan:

As his roommate, along with my cousin Michael we got to see CrazyLegs perform this eccentric dance in many settings with many partners, which were usually lissome girls from campus. One day we were hanging out in the living room eating pizza, burning yak butter, partying with friends when Crazylegs presented a floor show, making an entrance and humping his way crab-walking naked, upside down and backwards through the hall and into the living room with his naked and stoned girlfriend of the month riding him western style rocking in ecstasy

149

as he pumped her up. Our friends were amazed, but the CrazyLegs Camel Walk was something we had seen before and would see again.

One day I was driving home from school on Northern Blvd. passing the old Carvel near the City line when I stopped to pick up a couple of pretty hippy hitch-hikers. They admired the American Flag rolling paper that clad patriotic roaches in the ash-tray of my tan VW square back. We drove just another mile and went back to our launching pad in Bayside. We lit up fresh joints and paired off. I took blond haired Norwegian Carol. CLegs, who had been resting at home, took her eager brunette traveling companion named Joyce.

Carol was great company. Her ruddy sun-kissed complexion was darker than her light blond hair and she flushed scarlet red when she came. She had a dry sense of humor. In post coitus she said, "You made a liar out of me. I told you that I was Norwegian, but you made me Finnish". Then she took off her Playboy bunny golden coke-spoon pendant and hung it around my neck.

CLegs got along with his new match too. We went on a planned double date wherein with Carol, C-Legs and I arrived at the grand colonial house in Douglaston to pick up Joyce. We were struck when we entered the high-ceilinged foyer to notice that the golden oak floor was decorated with mahogany swastika inlays.

"Oy veh!" I said.

CrazyLegs did a wide-eyed slow take, turning his head like a thirsty dog trying to drink seltzer shocked by the exploding bubbles and suspicious of the effervescent buzz.

150

Carol was unperturbed in her Indian beaded headband and fringed buckskin skirt, as she was a frequent guest. She swung her head followed by her long blond hair, indicating that we should follow her and we did with some trepidation, through a broad parlor door across the threshold entering the formal dining room. Daddy looked at CLegs who was unmistakably a Jew and several years older than the average college sophomore. Dad's anger was seething as he informed us that his daughter was only fifteen. We had little patience with his self-righteousness. CLegs picked up his cue with perfect timing and informed Herr Barbi, "Age doesn't matter. Love is a totally individual thing. Affinity is all about the individual's vibration level. Your daughter has beautiful alpha wave vibes, man!"

Old Claus stood bolt upright from his dining room throne and nearly exploded in his retort: "Age matters to me!" and he pounded his fork and knife with clenched fists onto the polished wooden table, rattling the china, crystal, and silver.

We three "Gangsters of Love" soon found ourselves rapidly fleeing the premises with Joyce nimbly exiting a backyard window running across the slate patio, through the magenta azaleas and purple rhododendrons, and joining us as we accelerated in CLeg's froggy-looking slime-green Mercury Montego. We burned rubber and sped away to our Bayside lair, only a mile away.

Soon after this incident, returning home late one night, I was greeted in an overly familiar tone by a couple of plainclothes policemen or PI's who approached me and stood so close that I could smell cherry jelly donuts, coffee, and cigarettes on their co-mingled breaths. *Did they analyze my aroma too* I wondered. Could they smell the Sephardic pussy, blond-Lebanese hashish, and chocolate Carvel thick-shake on my moustache and in my breath? I guess I will never know that, nor exactly who these tough guys really were.

"Hey, Peter Pan, how you doing?"

There was no one else around. They were in my face and talking to me. "OK" I said.

"You live here, Pal?"

"Yeah."

"Where's Tinkerbell?"

"What?" I squinted at them, thinking, *what the fuck is this about?*

"Hey Pal, you like young girls?"

"Who are you?"

"We know you like 'em young. We know you and we know where you live, so be careful. I'm warning you, Pal. You never know who you're fucking with. OK?"

"Yeah. OK."

"OK?" He said it louder and meaner.

"I said OK. OK?"

They walked away into the otherwise quiet night.

That night I had been coming from my girlfriend on campus's dorm. She was my age, twenty. As I went upstairs and locked the door, I wondered if Carol was really nineteen, as she claimed. Was Joyce really fifteen? I didn't doubt that and didn't care. Those guys must have mistaken me for CrazyLegs. That would explain it; mistaken identity.

152

Who was Joyce's father and who were his friends? The age of at least one girl mattered very much to someone.

Politicos:

It was a political time and we were political people. We were not content to just beat the draft and make the most of our hedonistic impulses while attending college. We planned to take over the student government and control the one million dollar student activity fund. We wanted to have major rock concerts every weekend and use them as platforms to stimulate the community spirituality that was dormant in our apathetic classmates. With just a five minute pep-talk each week, while announcing our headliners, we could inspire and radicalize our music loving fellows into political action.

Action? Oh yes. We took action!

Cosmic Kitchen:

Unsatisfied with the dining plan and institutionalized food in our cafeteria AKA "Café Terrible", we started the "Cosmic Kitchen" as an alternative. With our new interdenominational chapel as head-quarters, using its catering kitchen to prep meals, we gave free natural food to as many as fifty people each day. About a dozen people showed up for the first meal, but it became popular, fast. We served brown rice, sautéed tofu and steamed veggies along with sunflower seeds and soy sauce. We had rice cakes and tahini, peanut butter, raisins, bananas and seasonal fruit like apples and oranges. We drank twig tea.

Our faculty sponsor was an energetic and androgynous contemporary literature teacher / feminist named Joan Frances. St. Joan helped us get other faculty members to contribute recipes and guest cook. Food was donated by local merchants including the "Stone Cellar" and "Food For Thought". We passed the hat to gather cash contributions for printing and frills like Macadamia nuts and dates. We added poetry readings and jam-sessions. "Cosmic Community" bulletins and announcements often developed into impromptu seminars. Our focus was peace, love, civil liberties and the end to the illegal and immoral so-called war in Vietnam.

Cosmic Chronicle:

The Cosmic Kitchen bulletin board developed into a newsletter called the Cosmic Chronicle. We published the Cosmic Chronicle using CrazyLegs's father's publishing equipment and distributed it free on campus. It grew incrementally from five hundred copies, to two thousand in our final edition. We had content including: "Swami Boogaloo Says", which was cosmic philosophy in small bites from our Swami. "Yoga Posture of the Day" was illustrated. "Recipe of the Day" was vegetarian. As resident theater critic, I used the platform for self-serving, dishy Campus Theater Reviews. We had guest columns from our leftist faculty. Everything was posted free including alternative public service announcements and bulletins. The Cosmic Chronicle was popular. Local merchants advertised including "Food For Thought", "My Father's Place" and our favorite, "Carvel" where we were regular customers. Revenue helped us grow. We were working towards a campus coup in the spring elections.

We also merchandised Cosmic Chronical T-shirts and "Vote for CrazyLegs" hash-pipes which we distributed mostly at concerts. Blond Lebanese and Nepalese Temple Balls were plentiful and these compact decorated tools worked well. They were used to expand community consciousness.

Along with ending the Vietnam War we demanded the legalization of marijuana and the release of all non-violent marijuana prisoners.

The First Annual End of the World Ball:

On a blustery winter's night, an inspired group of theater students staged "The First Annual End of the Year Ball!" We filled the chapel with revelers featuring a student band called "GOD". Entering the party which was already rocking without our usual cosmic entourage I heard for the first time The Band's recording of "The Shape I'm In". I danced my ass off with Mary Biggart, AKA Flash Hallucination, AKA Flash, AKA Kid Adventure, AKA Cocaine Mary. If Ike Turner could move like James Brown and he and Tina did a French style Apache dance, it might approximate the performance that Mary and I gave that night. I mopped the floor with her and swung her in the air. I did running jumps and sliding splits. Mary was shimmying and shaking, whirling and letting centrifugal force throw her antique hand-painted silk dress high enough to show that she was going "commando" with body paint for everyone to see. We cleared the floor and had a blast.

When the music slowed, we danced so close that our dripping sweat ran her body paint down her legs. We were in a state of blissful, psychedelic mutual adoration.

The other kids couldn't even wait for the music to quiet down or for our sweat to dry without asking us what we were on and how fast we could get them some of the same. I had it all wrapped up in foil packs in the laces of my red, white, and blue canvas dancing shoes and sold out my quota before the band plugged-in and took over the general mayhem and balled on.

It is great having the best stuff, but just like having a really hot girl-friend, it also tends to attract some of the wrong attention. Like people who want to party with you that you don't even know, when what they really want is to share your woman. People get desperate for coke and will track you down if they suspect that you have what they need. Even when you don't have it and I usually did not, once some people know that you did have the best, even just once, they keep going to you and expecting more. Sometimes no matter what you say, they think that you are just holding out and that can be such a drag. They are ready to trash your pad, beat you up, and rip you off. It is almost not worth getting into it because of the wrong people and the hassle it can bring. Unfortunately coke brings out the worst in people. Is it worth defending? I wish I had known before I got involved, but it seems that I had to learn it the hard way.

As the semester progressed so did our cosmic mission. Shortly before the elections for student council, the Chapel was vandalized and the Cosmic Kitchen was left in shambles. We suspected that we were the victims of misguided patriotic ass-holes. Not everybody was against the Vietnam War. Some people actually thought that we were Commie traitors. Maybe they were right. I sure wasn't rooting for General Westmoreland to beat Ho Chi Min and the Viet Cong. As the Cosmic

Kitchen was obviously the target of controversy, our dismayed Chaplain evicted us with respect and understanding, to avoid further damage to our resources.

It actually pissed us off quite a bit and we were disappointed that the Chaplain let the assholes succeed with violence. Standing up to the administration was too much for our otherwise cool chaplain. Too many Christian ministers embrace the meek aspect of Christianity. What would Jesus do?

Elect CrazyLegs:

At the student council Presidential election debate my cousin Michael was the audio-aid and controlled the loudspeaker system. As the various candidates made their boring perfunctory comments, the crowd grew to hundreds. It was a sunny spring day. The red, white, and blue bunting draped folding tables and a podium which had been placed for the event, in front of the red-brick Georgian style Humanities Building. The candidates were facing the great lawn which sloped upwards toward the Post Toastie Tudor Mansion and offices of our Dean and administrators. While my fellow students stretched and sunned in the cool spring breeze, I took the microphone for a loaded question:

"Listening to you candidates discuss the problem of student apathy is giving me student apathy. I wish I had some community spirituality. Can any one of you candidates say something that can turn me on?"

There were some hunched shoulders, raised eye-brows, frowns and negative head-nods before CrazyLegs boldly took the microphone and said, "Brother! Please come forward. Please come up here close to me at the podium."

I came forward as planned and stood with my hands in the pockets of my bell-bottomed hip-hugger jeans while CrazyLegs continued: "I know that you are concerned about student apathy and I share your feeling. None of us wants to continue the insane war in Vietnam and none of us wants to go to jail for what the bill of rights has guaranteed us in the Constitution. We are entitled to life, liberty, and the pursuit of happiness. That happiness precludes the insane and unenforceable prohibition of marijuana that has unfairly sent so many of our peaceful, non-violent brothers and sisters to jail.

Most of us are apathetic because we don't believe that we can do anything about this injustice. I believe that we can do something. I believe that we can do something really great! Would you like to do something really great, my brother?"

"Yes. Of course I want to do something great. I want to end the war and make marijuana legal, but how?"

"Would you be kind enough to reach under the bunting? I think that you will find something there that is really great, big enough to share and strong enough to turn everyone on."

I reached and found a six foot long joint that Michael and his techie friends had fashioned out of large cardboard commercial paper spools which they wrapped in red, white and blue paper, into which they inserted a huge Jamaican style spliff. I ceremoniously held it up over my head and CrazyLegs asked me to help him light it.

I heard a few excited exclamations behind me.

158

"Wow!"

"Holy Shit!"

"Far-fucking out!"

"Out-fucking rageous!"

I had been facing CrazyLegs and could not really see how much attention our typically apathetic class-mates were paying, but when I held up the joint I could hear the volume of exclamations and buzz developing. Soon it became hoops, applause and roaring approval. Our people had been awakened.

With the assistance of a guy named Steve Palay, who was a student activist, I held up the joint while CrazyLegs puffed and his cousin Billy waved a big flame from his Zippo around the tip until it glowed. Many of us blew and wet our fingers to tamp and stifle the flaming edges, until the giant joint was properly lit and smoking. Steve and Billy held it so that many students who were crowding the podium could take ceremonial tokes. Many other students started firing up their own stashes. We were having an impromptu "Smoke-In!"

Cousin Michael turned on CrazyLegs's theme song by the Rolling Stones, "Jumping Jack Flash", and cranked the volume up to maximum. Our raucous tribe shared the giant joint. CrazyLegs stripped out of his loose yogic clothes, swinging them over his head and throwing them to the crowd, like a stripper, revealing his slightly altered Superman Suit complete with blue tights, red cape and a big "C" on his chest. CrazyLegs got up onto the table and started to dance like an Egyptian, bending his elbows, turning his hands and proudly presenting his classic Semitic profile humping upward. Soon it was a dance party and then it was a freak parade.

This event attracted a previously underground and largely unknown gay cross-dressing constituency. They dressed up like drag-queens for the event. They fronted the parade in high camp vogue attitude parading up the hill to the Dean's office along with about a hundred stoked up freaks including, surprise, surprise, the "Damn Right Black Generation". What a warming and pleasant rush it gave us to see so many followers that we had not even imagined might be willing to join our cause. As we got to the administration building, Michael cut the music and turned on the bull-horn for CrazyLegs to address the Dean.

We Are the World:

"Dean Yazue! We know that you are in there hiding, so come out and face us. We are the students. We are the future. We are the now."

"Yeah! Come on out here and get stoned!" someone said.

"We demand that you legalize pot on CW Post Campus. Come on out and tell us that you are with us Dean Yazue!" CLegs continued.

"And no more finals!" said a student.

"Come out here and smoke this symbolic peace-pipe with us. We offer you peace and solidarity!" CLegs pleaded.

"End the War in Vietnam!" someone said.

"If you are truly our Dean, then join us. Smoke with us. Party with us! Dance with us! Be with us!" CLegs said.

"No more draft, motherfucker!" someone said.

"Right on!" said another.

160

CrazyLegs was earnest. He said, "Dean Yasue, we demand that you share our resolve to decriminalize marijuana. Make Post Campus safe haven for us students. Make us proud that you are our Dean. Tell the police that this is a safe-zone for marijuana and hashish! Tell the police that this is a private institution and to leave us the fuck alone."

"We do not need them!" another supporter said.

"Fuck no!" said another.

Bravo Cousin Michael!

Many fists were raised in protest and many oinking sounds were heard. Some of the oinking was amplified and disgusting. Cousin Michael was having fun! Although he stammered when speaking, it did not impair his ability to oink and make realistic farting sound effects. With amplification, he and his friends were impressive. It reflected diligent practice and their hard-work was appreciated by their boisterous undergraduate fellows.

Oinking was common at political demonstrations, but electronic amplification gave it an extra dimension. Michael and his friends made farting noises into the microphone which sounded juicy and offensive. Well done, Cousin Mike. Bravo! Encore! Some felt that these loud noises were gross, off-point and beneath the dignity of the substantial causes that we had championed. Some said that we were sophomoric. Then again, many of us were sophomores and for us it was great fun and age-appropriate. Some of us were falling down laughing. It was the funniest thing we had ever done, although I doubt that the Dean and campus security shared our great good humor. Well, maybe campus

161

security. Some of them were on the work-study program and were difficult to provoke and gratefully well known to cut us fellow students plenty of slack for our frequent infractions and gross misconduct.

"Out-fucking-rageous! Far-fucking-out! Oink! Oink! Fart! Fart!"

The Dean ignored us, or so it seemed, as he did not emerge to seize the moment.

Then we switched back to music and dancing. Mick Jagger was singing "Brown Sugar" when someone tapped me on the shoulder. I needed to be reminded that I was late for rehearsal down at the Theater. I was playing Kit Carson in "The Time of your Life" by William Saroyan for the American Theater Festival. Late I was. So I hustled down the hill and left the party at full-tilt and got into make-up and costume.

The Play is the Thing:

Was it a full tech dress rehearsal or preview? I hardly remember. The house was packed and it all went by like a blur. As I got ready to enter the stage as the buckskin wearing, gray-haired, pot-bellied, spell-binding barroom storyteller, the prop manager strapped some new paraphernalia around my waist. There was a canteen, a mess kit, knife-fork-and-spoon set, and bull Durham pouch. I sauntered on stage and pulled up a spindle backed chair, turned it around and straddled it sitting hard on the eating utensils, sticking myself in the right testicle with the fork. There was silence and everyone was looking at me. *My cue?*

"Did I ever tell you about the time I was married to a midget just thirty-nine inches tall?"

I bantered on in perfect character and accent. Unfortunately it was Act II Scene 3 and I was doing Act III Scene 2 or some similar juxtaposition of the script. Gary Swanson, the star that I was cast to support, had a shocked look in his steely blue eyes. He was too cool to panic and he tried prompting me back to the act on stage with leading questions like,

"Hey weren't you telling me about a fella by the name of Rufus Jenkins? Did you used to know a guy with six white horses and two black ones?"

While we were rewriting Saroyan's masterpiece we were giving wrong cues to the rest of our mixed college and professional cast. The light crew was moving spots around the stage as though they were searching for an escaped convict in a prison movie.

"Yadda, Yadda, Warden! Yadda, yadda, you bulls! I had a head full of Lenny Bruce. I was so stoned.

Sailors were following floozies and bar-flies into the bathroom which the audience found hilarious. There were more characters coming out of the bathroom than clowns piling out of a Volkswagen Bug at the Ringling Brothers and Barnum and Bailey Circus.

I was on a roll, although, I was not actually cast as the star.

We kept in character and finally got back to the proper act and scene. Unfortunately with all the stress this extemporaneous rewrite caused we robbed thirty years of life from David Scanlon. He was our director who was just in from Reed College. He was heading our department. This was his LIU Post directorial debut. He gave me the big break and wanted to be my mentor. May he rest in peace.

Consequences:

At intermission, our star grabbed me by the throat and terrified me with death threats and hissing invective. This performance was his big break. His fiancée's father, Sandy Becker, the children's entertainer, TV star and impresario was in the audience watching. Gary accused me of tripping on LSD and ruining his hard work. Actually I had snorted a bit of coke backstage, just to sharpen up after an exhausting all-nighter, next day and afternoon binge of assorted radical activities. That would not have been of any consolation to him so I just denied the LSD part, which was not exactly the absolute and perfect truth either. Nothing I could have said would have replayed the upsetting on-stage blunder. Even though the audience liked it, it was an upsetting mistake, totally unprofessional and he was furious.

In retrospect, I can empathize with poor Gary's aggravation. After all, Sandy Becker was a huge star. He was like the Jerry Lewis of children's programming. I used to love the way he danced when he did "Hambone." I am sure that his Hambone character influenced CrazyLegs and maybe "Silly-Walking" John Cleese too, of whom we had not yet had the pleasure. Poor Gary, he did not yet know that he would marry Sandy Becker's daughter and become a successful working actor after all.

Act III:

The second half of the play went even better than the first half, as we stuck to Saroyan's script. After the final curtains went down we held hands and bowed to wild applause. It was a terrific play. We replayed it as written for ten performances. It got better and better every show.

But back on the night with my disruptive improvisation, Lee, the lighting designer who was a visiting professional told me that my performance was priceless. He also invited me back to his place in Greenwich Village for a hot-oil massage which I refused suspecting that it might be leading into an uninvited and unwanted gay proposition. I wonder if he really liked my performance. I like to think so.

Paranoid?

Soon after the big improvisation, I was called before the "TABS" committee. I don't remember what the letters actually stood for, but it was a special investigation committee. It had only been called once before. That was just before I reached campus as a freshman. The Nassau County cops had busted seventy-one students as part of "Operation Big Wheel". Mostly fine art students were busted for marijuana related misdemeanors and felonies. That bust had decimated the Theater Department. The remaining kids were still in shock. They were so paranoid, that they treated me like I was a narc, when I first arrived.

My early casting in lead parts only fueled their suspicion. They really disliked me when they found out that I was balling the head of Thespian's girl-friend. She didn't tell me that she was already taken when she seduced me in dance class and I didn't stop screwing her until some months later, when I found someone that I liked better, my acting teacher's daughter.

My acting teacher was directing the next play. Since the daughter was not much of a looker it was assumed that I was just an opportunist, sexing up to get "in" with her Bohemian mother. They did not know it, but the

165

plain looking daughter had a lovely voice and the most electric sense of touch that I have ever experienced. If she did not turn out to be a lesbian, I might have continued the relationship even after her mother's play was done. But, perceptions being what they are, I am afraid that I did not make many friends and I soon learned that I would be needing as many friends as I could get.

The TABS committee had heard that I took LSD before the American Theater Festival performance and that I had bragged to more than one anonymous witness that I was "fucking out of sight, Baby!" I am not sure that that was something I would say and I felt that the charge was bogus.

No one believed me when I denied the allegations and my accusers remained anonymous, despite my demands that they come forward. That anonymity pissed me off! It might have been true that the report had actually been made, but I honestly had no recollection of the offensive remark. I used to drink irresponsibly back then. I did it with the encouragement of the faculty to help me develop the alcoholic character, Kit Carson. I had a bit of trouble distinguishing between the character and the "actor in charge". I was renting in Northport, living with Cocaine Mary and visiting Jack Kerouac's favorite bar. I did it without costume but in character and just tried my crazy lines. No harm done, that I can recall. The things that happened to me and the things that I did while under the influence of alcohol are the hardest for me to remember. The memories that I do retrieve involving alcoholic incidents are the most unreliable.

My father once referred me to the Talmud by saying, "If a man wants to beat a dog, he will find a stick."

I think it applied in my case with these proceedings.

Norm Seider was my film teacher and head of the department. After reviewing two of my papers in which I interviewed Viva Superstar and Joe Franklin, Norm called me "the Tom Wolff of the campus circuit..." He told me that he wanted to make a film with me. He wanted to mentor me. Norm was the grand inquisitor for TABS committee that day and he pressed the charges. Whom can you trust?

My acting teacher, Frank Scaringi, who was also Rodney Dangerfield's lawyer, manager and partner, played the bar-tender in "The Time of Your Life". He was a terrific character actor and popular on campus. He was also the model on which Rodney based his comedy lawyer, Vinny Pumpaniece. He didn't pump any nephews, just nieces and that included half the freshman theater department. I had thought he was my friend, but he turned on me like a bad dog. He testified that I tried to kill him by throwing a wooden clog at him during acting class. He told me to really let go and show him some anger. Or did he ask me to "shoe him some anger?" That dirty rat. I showed him anger but he did not appreciate it.

My dance teacher, Cliff Keuter, actually caught me smoking hash in the locker room with my fellow male dancers. We were making fun of his oversized cod-piece. He was standing right behind me while I carried on about the ridiculous costume. The gay guys were giving me wormy looks and couldn't stop laughing. Then I realized that Cliff was standing behind me catching my act but not laughing. But, I give Cliff all the credit in the world because even after that, he stuck up for me. No pun intended. He told the committee that my behavior off-stage was none of his concern. It had nothing to do with dance class or the dance shows in which I performed with his direction. What mattered was that I had never missed a cue and always hit my marks. He had no complaints to register. Bravo, Cliff. It was his last year in the department.

It was planned that I be expelled from school and I had to wonder if I was really being punished for messing up my cue in dress-rehearsal or if it was political. We had recently closed Northern Blvd., and faced down the Brookville Police to protest the latest most atrocious incident in Vietnam. I forget which one. Or was it all the Cosmic Stuff. Kids I didn't even know were calling me "Cosmic Steve". TABS was making me paranoid. I thought that my professors liked me and they were all, except for Cliff chipping in with their own stories and accounts of my most dubious moments under their supervision.

It turned out OK. The TABS committee decided not to throw me out of school. That was a relief because I was in the process of trying to overturn my 1A draft status and get a student deferment. Expulsion would have put me a bit closer to a difficult choice between Vietnam, Federal Prison, or fugitive status in Mexico, Canada, or Sweden where I didn't know anyone. That was in the back of my mind and it bothered me for the thirty months that I had been classified "IA". I had passed my physical and the military did not think I was crazy. Not too crazy for the insanity they had in mind. That classification and threat had a lot to do with some of my excessive choices regarding substance abuse. I believed that if I really did go crazy, I might not have to do something really evil and sick, like go to Vietnam and kill innocent Asians. Somebody tell me again. What is sane and what is crazy?

The theater department evidently needed me and showed some mercy. The "Time of Your Life" had a ten show run to play and we didn't have an understudy for my character, Kit Carson. I had a prominent role in the dance show and I was the subject of a students' group film final project. My punishment was that TABS would be watching me and that in my next year, which was my senior year, I was to be banned from the main stage.

Going Straight:

So I went home to Bayside and started waking up straighter and going to school without smoking any pot or taking anything stronger than coffee. I went to a shrink for a while because I was feeling stressed-out and paranoid. He prescribed valium to help me keep focused on my studies. I was a Dean's List student and had fifteen to eighteen credits per semester. That required going to class and reading more than I had time for. I also worked part-time jobs when I wasn't working in the theater. When I didn't take the valium on time, I got the shakes, so I quit the drug and the shrink within a couple months.

Legal Drugs:

I remember going on stage straight when I had quit valium. When I had to say my first line, I felt like I couldn't start the first syllable. My head felt like it was on my neck too tight and that it would was creaking and crunching when I rotated it. Is that stage-fright? I never used to have it. I always loved to get on stage to sing, dance, act, play. This was different. I think it was valium withdrawal. I can't believe that some people take that stuff to get high. It had the opposite effect on me.

Valium was like "Stay-Straight". It brought me right down. Valium is addictive. It really makes you wonder about the Food and Drug Administration and the choices that they try to enforce regarding public health and safety.

After I got into the first syllable, I squeezed out the word and by that time, an eternal instant, believe me, the stage-fright was gone and I was back "in the zone", not the Twilight Zone, the zone, zone, where everybody wants to be.

I changed my derelict habits which had started when I was fifteen. At the ripe old age of twenty-one, I was partially reformed, saving my hard partying and binging for after school, weekends, and vacations. While I no longer recommend cannabis, LSD, or magic mushrooms, at least they are not addictive. With some will power, they are quittable. Back then, I would have recommended these substances to everyone, but not LSD and mushrooms. They require some discretion, but I still wish that someone would have dosed the water coolers with LSD for the White House and Congress. I believed that it would have made the world a better place.

Say What?

One day I came home to Bayside and found Cousin Michael and my girl-friend Yma, AKA "Yma the Schema" listening to Wes Montgomery. They were grooving on "Down Here on the Ground". My intimates of whom I felt somewhat protective were sniffing heroin with an unknown African American who appeared to be a few years older than us.

"Hey man. I really dig your record collection. You got some great taste man. You dig Miles."

"Get out of here." I said.

"Yeah, man. You got a fine lady, here," he said.

"Get outta here!" I said again with intensity.

"Oh yeah…and, and, and, I gotta taste for you too, man."

"Get, get, get the fuck outta here. You Asshole! Get out of here before I throw you down the stairs and tell the cops to take you away."

My cousin Michael who stammered suggested that I be cool and Yma went to the bathroom. I told Michael to shut the fuck up before I told his mother on him. I was supposed to be watching out for him. Geez.

Our jazz loving interloper finally took the hint and said,

"OK. You be like that, Baby. I was invited here. No need for you to be going off."

He got up and calmly left.

That's Tellin 'Em!

When CrazyLegs heard about this incident he was strongly supportive of my intervention. He even wrote a column in the Cosmic Chronicle signed "anonymous" suggesting that heroin dealers discovered on campus be thrown off the rooftops as strong discouragement like good citizens were doing in Harlem.

I agreed with CLegs to some degree. I was against capital punishment and killing. Throwing dealers from rooftops would likely be fatal. Unfortunately, the black drug dealers whom it threatened, based on the previous incident assumed that I wrote the uncool article. I received numerous threats on the phone, through messengers and menacing gestures from dark skinned men that I did not know, but who seemed to know me.

It appeared that the black drug dealers thought that I was protecting turf. I was not a drug dealer. This is the kind of thing I mentioned earlier. If you ever get the best stuff, users never forget that you are the man. I had actually been approached by black dealers and basically offered a job distributing hard drugs to white kids. They thought that they knew me, but they were wrong. Much as I favored legalization of pot, hash and psychedelics, I was dead set against ups and downs. I hadn't learned yet how bad coke could be, but I was against heroin and I was against them getting my friends hooked. I was also against them turning my girl-friends into heroin addicted prostitutes.

Paranoid? Is there something to be paranoid about?

I had to start arming myself for mid-night walks from the theater along spacious lawns, formal gardens, and through broad open parking lots to my girl-friend's dorm room. This had been my Garden of Eden. I carried a semi-gravity knife in my boot, which I had previously only used to skin and slice apples, oranges, pears, and mangoes. Now I practiced often in front of the mirror, drawing the knife, flipping the blade and slashing like a Jet, from West Side Story. Where was *my* gang? *Paging Jerome Robbins. Paging Leonard Bernstein. Please report to the parking lot outside Brookville Hall.* In my sleeve I carried a lead pipe within a rolled newspaper which I had read about in Charles Mingus's autobiography, "Beneath the Underdog". Being prepared worked. Fortunately I never had to test my pacifism and these weapons remained unused.

Good-bye Cousin Mike:

This heroin business with Yma was not the only time I had been fed up with Cousin Michael. He and his friends robbed a hospital one night and came back with a life-time supply of laughing gas and downers. Many nights he and his juvenile delinquent (JD) friends would get so stoned that they would knock over the gas tank in his bed room and Spiros, the landlord who lived downstairs with his young family would want to know. "What a hell going on up there?"

"Dumbbells!" I would say.

"Dumbbells!" What a dumbbells?"

"It is Michael. He is working out with too much weight. He dropped his dumbbell! Sorry."

One night I came home and told him stop knocking over the tank. My erstwhile girl-friend, Norwegian Carol, fell out of the closet naked and laughing. I guess the joke was on me, somehow.

Eventually I did call his Mom, my Aunt Ann and she was ready to kill the messenger, me, but I did manage to get rid of him by semester's end.

Good-bye CrazyLegs:

One day I came home and CrazyLegs was on two telephones watching all three of our TV's which he had stacked up on each other in the living room. He was also listening to the radio. It was all sports and he was going crazy betting. I had never seen this side of my friend before, but I soon discovered that CLegs was a compulsive gambler. He ran up such a big debt with his bookie that he had to blow town, fast. I have never seen him since. I heard from Lily Lovely that her brother was still in contact and that he was in the promo T-shirt advertising specialty biz up around Boston/Cambridge.

After C-Legs split, I got stiffed with a huge phone bill. His mother came to pick up his stuff and that was the only time we ever met. She wouldn't pay the bill and I had to close the account, which, like the lease was in my name. To reopen the account, with a thick accent I told the phone company that Steve had been drafted and that I was his Polish cousin Zavel. With a thirty dollar deposit, they dropped the old charges of about one hundred sixty and opened the account in my name, Zavel Carlinsky, which they listed in the directory, at 42-12 203rd St.

CrazyLegs and I did not end the war in Vietnam, or legalize marijuana, but we had fun trying, kicking the establishment hard in the ass every chance we got.

CATCH 23

During the winter and spring of 1969, and especially between my greetings from Uncle Sam until I showed up at Fort Hamilton for my physical, I did my best to qualify for a 4F or at least the more temporary 1Y psychological deferment. My protocol included ingesting mega-doses of high-voltage purple barrel LSD, 1000mg per pill, broken and swallowed in quarters and halves, to boost new peaks from diminishing plateaus, postponing the deep crashes and jingle-jangle mornings, which were inevitable and required chain-smoking marijuana just to settle my nerves. You would think that would have been enough, but wait, there was more. That acid was laced with enough speed to drive manic benders for days into nights, which flashed by like strobe lights and put me outside myself, watching my life like a flickering old-time movie, with day-glow color and fun-house mirror filters. My traveling- companion/roommate and dear friend Dave was winning the Hugh O'Brien award for acting at UCLA, while I was making enough money selling baby pictures to housewives to keep our Santa Monica Beach-party playing at full tilt boogie. So, ripped as we were, we were functional; highly functional. That ended when I flew back to NY to meet the draft board.

When Dave and I were together, I managed to keep us out of trouble. Our neighbor, Diane was a stripper to put her boyfriend through law-school. He became John DeLorean's attorney and helped David in his time of need. As neighbors, we visited each other and enjoyed playing cards, smoking pot and having the time of our life. Dave, who was born on Christmas, became Jesus on acid. He also became Oedipus, Hamlet,

Alexander the Great, and did Napoleon, just for laughs. Jesus brought out the hippy in him, and he liked to take off his bathing suit to greet the revolution. He qualified for 4F, but when he tried to go outside, I blocked the door and reminded him that the revolution was just inside with us; not outside in the cruel world.

Phone calls were expensive but we stayed in touch enough for me to know that 129 Frazer Avenue had drawn many old friends to take residence in my bedroom. That was June 1969. I had not been in touch for at least a month and don't remember how I finally got through, but when I spoke to David, I was shocked to learn that he had gone outside naked and been reported by the Psychology Professor who lived on our block. Police came and dragged naked, tripping, Jesus off to jail, just as he had prophesied. He spent thirty days in LA City Jail being gang-raped until he escaped and got put into a psych ward. The punishment was cruel and usual, in our minimal justice system, and the torture was amplified by the LSD. He was never the same.

When we got together, we resumed our tripping ways in CA where he went back to UCLA without missing a credit. In Brookville, where I was attending LIU Post as acting major, David visited me and our trip raged on, even as I starred in 27 Wagon Loads of Cotton, in the Little Theater, on campus. I wondered how it was that David spent thirty days in jail and none of our high school buddies, who were sharing the house contacted me, or used their parents' connections to help him. Were they afraid of getting busted too? It still bothers me that even though we were all friends, none of them would explain it to me. Did they have group amnesia? Karen, who moved into David's bedroom with us before I left, had

176

nothing to say. She was wonderful and loving, but I imagine overwhelmed by the boys that came. She died young and I never got to hear her story. Dick and Jed who came together were useless. Jed got my motorcycle and my room. He would have been the one to interview, but he eluded me and also died young. Dick totally avoided me and Robby was likewise useless for my inquiry, playing dumb to perfection. Our friend Dave suffered so much. His doctors gave him lithium but he missed the manic highs. He spent thirty days in hell and nobody helped get him out. I was three thousand miles away, oblivious to his incarceration and absorbed in obstructing my own invitation to hell in Vietnam.

The bus was waiting in front of the Elks Lodge in Great Neck. I was happy to see Bobby Bliss from my high school class among those waiting to board. We sat next to each other. As the bus rolled to Fort Hamilton we smoked hash and examined each other's notes from psychiatrists which were common among us middle-class draft resisters. Bobby's note was surprising. His insane creds were much stronger than mine, and yet, he seemed much more afraid than I was of what we would experience at the fort. My report was developed from analysis derived by Dr. Prenski, after seventeen hours of psychological testing. He called it a full psychological profile taken over two consecutive days. I tripped on mescaline for the first half of the test and did all the algebra in my head. He told me I could be a rocket scientist or brain surgeon. My father was with me for the evaluation and was stunned to learn that I was so smart. I thought Prenski was giving me another psychological test because I didn't know that I was that smart either. I had dropped out of school when I was sixteen; a flop in academics. He concluded that my borderline personality was so averse to authority that the stress of military discipline would likely make my behavior unmanageable and potentially violent. I don't remember how he put it, but that was the gist, and he assured my father and me that he was batting one thousand. Every single youth that he recommended for psychological deferment was deferred.

I was feeling cocky with a captive audience on the bus. I started singing Arlo Gurthrie's "Alice's Restaurant" song and encouraged everyone to sing along. Not even Bobby felt that high. "You can get anything you want, at Alice's restaurant, excepting Alice. You can get anything you want at Alice's Restaurant." I could tell that the audience was not with me, but I was a trooper and continued trying with the force of my personality to win them over. "You can get anything that you want," It seemed appropriate to me and much more clever than the camp song about one hundred bottles of beer on the wall or the one about a dog named Bingo, but I had not considered that some of my bus-mates were volunteers, joining the army without being drafted. They wanted to go to Vietnam and could hardly wait to start killing Communists. A record of military service was useful for ambitious young men who might seek careers in politics. To my thinking, they were insane or stupid, but I discovered that they were not insensitive and that my singing was pissing them off. "Shut the fuck up, you pinko-commie-faggot-asshole." I am sure they meant me. They were wrong about the faggot part and they forgot to include Jew which usually went along with the rest. Considering their raw anger and our close quarters, I decided to stop singing. "Asshole," I heard it again. I guess someone was still mad. I have that

178

effect on some people. The fear and anxiety of the situation ruined the hashish buzz. I was a hero to no one, not even Bobby Bliss. He sat next to me with a case of the jitters. The bus ride was too long, and no fun at all.

When we arrived, soldiers steered us into a large room with many tables and military personnel stationed at each one. We were told to strip down to our underpants. We were broken into groups for testing. During the hearing test, we were instructed to press a button when we heard a tone and to release it when the tone became inaudible. I was in booth number four. To fail, I did not press the button until the tone was loud. When it started to fade, I released the button. An angry sergeant said, "Who is the clown in booth number four?" Louder and standing right behind me he shouted, "Who is the clown in number four?"

I turned around and faced him but said nothing. "Did you not hear me?" He said.

"What?" I answered. Nobody was laughing.

"I want you, boot. I am going to make a man out of you and enjoy every minute of it."

"What?" I said.

I don't remember all the tests that we had and that I failed, but something about the confrontation with Sergeant Testosterone and the hashish I had been smoking and the after effect of the mescaline I had taken the day before had me in an extroverted mood. I went totally into Randle P. McMurphy mode, as in "One Flew Over The Cuckoo's Nest" which I had been considering for an audition piece. I was feeling it. Remember he goes into the psycho ward and says, "Who is the chief bull-

goose looney here?" That's how I felt during the physical at Fort
Hamilton. Everybody was crazy except for me. I had a belly full of the
bellicose sergeant. "Hey Sarge" I said. "If you really did manage to get
me over in Vietnam and you gave me a gun, you would be the first one I
would kill. I am hoping that our team loses because I admire Ho Chi Min.
I think the Viet Cong are cool and that Americans don't belong over there
at all." He put his nose right next to my nose. I was scared but the hash
kept me cool. "You are not even my boss, Sarge. I am a civilian. That
war is illegal and immoral. Don't you know that?" I felt like the hero to
all the nervous teenagers standing in the underpants being afraid. I am
glad that the volunteers didn't jump me. Even though the draft evaders
outnumbered the volunteers and military personnel, I doubt that anyone
would have defended me. Think about the way thousands of Jews went
into gas chambers, bullied by handfuls of armed Nazis. It happened over
and over again. Millions were killed that way. The insanity continued. If
they only knew that they could have overwhelmed their captors and would
not have all died trying. Fewer would have died.

Inside the Army Psychiatrist's office I answered boilerplate questions
about my mother and father. I shared my fantasies. "If I had to fight? I
would continue the revolution of Che Guevara and fight to liberate Latin
America." I likened President Nixon to the Sheriff of Nottingham and
myself to Robin Hood. His questions were clichés and my off the cuff
answers were just not too nutty to get passed his pre-conceived notion that
I was sane enough to be trying to get out by reason of insanity. My case
was so common. What a lot of crazy shit.

After all the testing was over and we had our clothes back on, I found my name listed on a sheet of paper posted on a wall. I had passed the physical. I was 1A. That is the worst. 1A means fit for service. I could be activated and sent to basic training in weeks. I was so pissed that I re-entered the shrink's office. He had a nervous teenager in his underpants sitting in a chair while he interviewed him from a plush chair behind his desk. The kid looked scared and the doctor seemed startled to see me. I barged in and picked up a brass torchiere from beside his desk and lifted it over my head like a dumbbell. "How crazy do I have to be to get out of this motherfucking pig-shit army?" I said it as loud as I could. Then I threw the lamp hard across his desk. It flew passed his head and smashed against the wall behind him, taking down a couple of glass framed diplomas, as collateral damage. The shrink yelled, "Orderly. Orderly." Two black men in white suits entered the room. "Get this guy out of here."

The orderlies looked at me and then looked at each other. Their eyes were slow and glassy. The doctor might have interrupted a staff pot party in the lounge. The chubbier one spoke, "OK, baby. Let's be cool. Everything is going to be alright."

I bolted past them and ran down the hall. I had hashish in my pocket. I ran into a men's room and hid my little metal pipe along with my stash in the toilet paper roll inside a booth. Then I flushed the toilet and washed my hands pretending to be making a normal pit stop. I was being cool after the chase. I reentered the hall and found the orderlies waiting for me. Without further resistance, I allowed them to walk me out the building and down the street to the gates of the Fort, in Bay Ridge Brooklyn, right near the Verrazano Bridge. I had missed the bus and hitch-hiked home.

Acting crazy during the Army physical was the most important part I had ever played and I blew it. All that tripping on LSD, Mescaline, Psilocybin, magic mushrooms, Hawaiian Woodrose, DMT, hash and pot had made me sane enough to serve. I had heard about Catch 22 which made anyone who wanted to get a psychological deferment fit for duty, because avoiding service was sane. That was the essence of catch 22. I was so crazy and they were so desperate that I was an ideal draftee. The sergeant really wanted me and insane was good enough in 1969. That was catch 23.

DRAFT RESISTER
BY STEVE SLOANE

"Uncle Sam broke a lot of hearts and minds in Viet Nam. This popular image was ubiquitous in 1969, when "Draft Resister takes place, Uncle Sam has more than half a million soldiers, mostly drafted against their will. Once in the service these young men, some too young to buy cigarettes and beer, and too young to vote are routinely ordered to fight an illegal, immoral, unnecessary war.

Steve Sloane, narrator, writer, burned his draft card at an SDS rally in New Paltz election night 1968 and went underground, traveling from parties, to demonstrations, to crash pads, landing in Santa Monica California, where he non-matriculated in theatre and film at UCLA, working day jobs and finding a marketable skill as a door to door salesman. Discovered by his draft board, he returned to NY and was reclassified 1A, and amazingly passed his physical. Pro-bono Quaker anti-war lawyers assisted in appealing his dangerous status for 30 months while he attended LIU Post majoring in acting. A lucky lottery number gave his personal drama a happy ending.

Mina Daniel is a new face in the New York City acting scene. This Botswana-born Angolan actress grew up in Philadelphia, and found her love for performance while attending Penn State University. In season 2 of the hit comedy webseries "The Loiuse Log" Mina played the role of the mini-van's alter ego. Roger Ebert confirmed that it looked like Chrysler's "whisper commercial" had been inspired by The Louise Log episode Mina was featured in.

Benjamin Strate
Acting: Kathryn Pogson (Stanislavski); Aoife Smythe (Stanislavski/Meisner); Zoe Waites (Classical); Polly Hootkins (On-Camera Technique); Julie Boyd (Stanislavski); David Loud (Musical Theatre); Simon Dormandy (Audition Technique); Deborah Kym (Audition Technique)
Voice: Simon Money (Theatre); Nick Dicola (Speech and Dialect); David

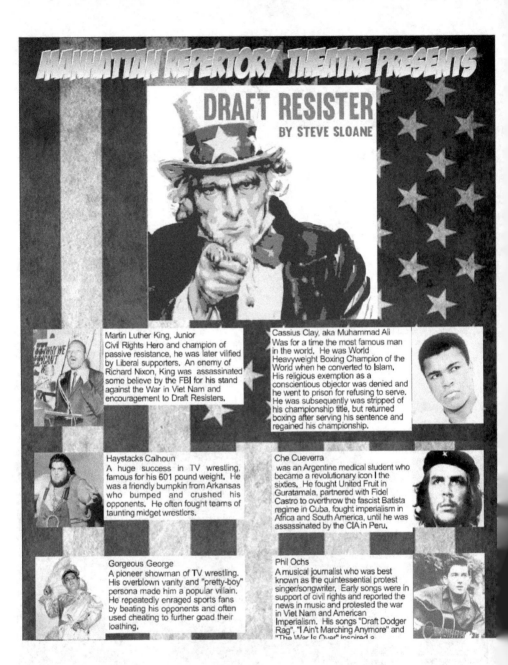

DRAFT RESISTER
BY STEVE SLOANE

Martin Luther King, Junior
Civil Rights Hero and champion of passive resistance, he was later vilified by Liberal supporters. An enemy of Richard Nixon, King was assassinated some believe by the FBI for his stand against the War in Viet Nam and encouragement to Draft Resisters.

Cassius Clay, aka Muhammad Ali
Was for a time the most famous man in the world, He was World Heavyweight Boxing Champion of the World when he converted to Islam, His religious exemption as a conscientious objector was denied and he went to prison for refusing to serve. He was subsequently was stripped of his championship title, but returned boxing after serving his sentence and regained his championship.

Haystacks Calhoun
A huge success in TV wrestling, famous for his 601 pound weight, He was a friendly bumpkin from Arkansas who bumped and crushed his opponents. He often fought teams of taunting midget wrestlers.

Che Cueverra
was an Argentine medical student who became a revolutionary icon I the sixties, He fought United Fruit in Guratamala, partnered with Fidel Castro to overthrow the fascist Batista regime in Cuba, fought imperialism in Africa and South America, until he was assassinated by the CIA in Peru.

Gorgeous George
A pioneer showman of TV wrestling. His overblown vanity and "pretty-boy" persona made him a popular villain. He repeatedly enraged sports fans by beating his opponents and often used cheating to further goad their loathing.

Phil Ochs
A musical journalist who was best known as the quintessential protest singer/songwriter, Early songs were in support of civil rights and reported the news in music and protested the war in Viet Nam and American Imperialism. His songs "Draft Dodger Rag", "I Ain't Marching Anymore" and "The War Is Over" inspired a

DRAFT RESISTER (A play in one act)

Curtains open:

Narrator: "April 4th, 1969 is a cool gray morning in Crenshaw District, south Los Angeles. It is the first anniversary of Martin Luther King, Junior's assassination. No cars are driving on the streets. Nobody is walking on the sidewalks. A dented and dirty candy cane colored hula hoop is on the tiny dry patchy brown grass lawn. A tipped over baby blue tricycle is by the neighbor's doorway. A yellow plastic pale is upside down and a matching shovel is by its side next to the blue aluminum mail-box on a wooden post. "

(A young, skinny, long-haired, pale skinned salesman wearing a borrowed leather jacket with patch pockets and thin lapels parks a small red motorcycle on its kickstand. He takes a clipboard from the bikes luggage rack. He has long legs and thick rubber soled tan work boots. His walk is slinky as he leads with a big foot swinging his long body to follow. He pauses to listen to a distant cornet playing the slow blues from a neighbor's house. The song, 'A Letter From Vietnam.' The music rests and a big dog howls a reply.)

No more narration. (The salesman walks up the short concrete path to a door. With two knuckles, he knocks a classic pattern that resembles Woody Woodpecker's be-bopping rhythm-*knock-diddy knock-knock*. No answer. He knocks again. No answer. He turns his back and takes a few steps away. A woman remains out of sight but answers through a narrow opening in the door.

"Who's there?"

185

"Ma'am. This is Hollywood International Color Studios."

"What?"

"Hollywood International Color Studios and they are conducting a television and marketing research survey."

"Who?"

"Ma'am. They would like to know what your favorite channel is on TV."

(Door opens more.)

"Why are you bothering me, son?"

"Ma'am. This is a television and marketing research survey and they would like to know what your favorite channel is on TV."

"So?"

"So, what is your favorite channel?"

"Well, I like to watch the wrestlers on channel six."

"OK. That is good. Channel six for wrestlers." (He jots a note on his clipboard.)

"Yeah, I like to watch them fight."

"OK. That is good. When you shop in the supermarket, do you prefer store brand or name brand products?"

"Yeah, I like to see Haystacks Calhoun fight all the little midgets."

"Excuse me, Ma'am, we can get back to wrestling, but..."

She says "That country boy, he is so fat, but you know he is handsome and nice and friendly and all. He calls everybody 'Cousin' 'Hey Cousin! Howdy Cousin. Howdy. This here's the Haystacks. Haystacks Calhoun and I am as big as I want to be. You think I'm fat, but you better not laugh at me, Cousin, or I'll sit on you and make you sorry. And you know what, Cousins? I hate me some little midgets.' Oh, he is so funny. He's

186

just about to squash the midgets, but the midgets are just too fast and they always get away. Then they tease him and make him chase. They are some mean little midgets. I wish Haystacks would squash one or maybe two. It would serve them right."

"Ma'am, do you prefer the name brands or the store brands?"

"Happy Humphrey is even bigger than Haystacks."

"Ma'am?"

"I know. Haystacks weighs 601 pounds and Happy Humphrey's 750!"

"Ma'am?

"That's right. But Haystacks has more muscle and Happy Humphrey is just a big butterball."

"Name brand or store brand?"

"When are they going to have them fight each other?"

 "So, do you prefer name brand or store brand?"

"What you mean store brand name brand?"

"Ma'am, would you open the door a little wider so that I can see what products you have in your house and then I can tell you whether you have store brand or name brand?" (The door opens and the overcast light reveals a tired looking woman of thirty-five clutching the throat of her housedress, which reaches mid-calf. She has droopy dark mid-calf socks and open toed sandals. Her complexion is milk-chocolate and her hair is covered with a red cowboy scarf. Inside is a small living room with a mantle and a gas fireplace. The room has beige carpet and ruby velvet matching couch, loveseat, and easy chair. Furniture crowds around the fireplace, which has a large cabinet style TV in front of it. A rectangular glass coffee table in front of the couch matches the end tables next to the love seat and big chair. It is obvious that the fireplace is unused and that the TV is the center of attention. On the wall behind the TV is a large framed portrait of a handsome young soldier. The room opens into an open kitchen. It has a yellow counter with brown cushioned leatherette bar stools. Past them are avocado green appliances with white linoleum flooring. A shelf above the sink on the far wall is visible from the front door. An ironing board is open in the kitchen with a steam iron sitting up and ready.

The salesman enters and stands near her as she seems to be sniffing him suspiciously. She walks upstage from him as he stands near the entrance. Across the neat living room he looks over her shoulder into the kitchen and sees a box of Brillo and a bottle of Ivory Snow Dish Washing Liquid on the sink).

"Ma'am. I see that you have a bottle of Ivory Soap. That is a name brand product. Can you identify another brand name product that you bought recently?"

Looking into the kitchen, she says "I have a box of Brillo".

"Brillo? That is great. Can you bring it to me?"

"Yes. OK." She gets the Brillo.

"Would you please give me the box-top?"

She rips off the box-top and hands it to the young man.

"What is your name, Ma'am?"

"My name is Lily. Lily Johnson."

(Pressing his ballpoint pen and using his clip board, he writes her name on the box top as he speaks.) "Mrs. Johnson. You are a winner! That is right. Brillo, in conjunction with Hollywood International Color Studios is

188

awarding you a prize. You have won a beautiful 5 X 7 inch full color portrait like this." He opens a folder and shows her a picture of an adorable Afro-American baby boy. "That's right, Mrs. Johnson. Frank Williams, one of Hollywood's finest photographers will come right here to your house so that you won't have to bother going downtown in the traffic to the studio. Frank will come right here and photograph you or your loved ones. "

"Oh, well. Who would I take a picture of? I don't have any babies anymore."

"Well. Who is that handsome young soldier?" He indicates a photo on the mantle.

"Oh. He's my son, John."

"Well, Mrs. Johnson, why don't you make an appointment with me to have Frank Williams shoot a nice portrait of you and you can send it to your young man? Imagine how happy he would be to have a fine new picture of his pretty young mother."

"Oh. I don't think so. My Johnny was killed in Vietnam."

"Oh. I am sorry to hear that. That is tragic. I am so sorry. Such a handsome boy. I am sorry for your loss."

"He didn't want to fight. He didn't want to go. He got drafted and then he got killed."

"I am sorry. I wish he didn't go. It is a sad story and much too common. I wish nobody went."

"How come you aren't over there in Vietnam, fighting? How come my boy is dead and you are here? I guess white boys don't have to go and die, like my black boy, Johnny."

189

"Well, Mrs. Johnson, I am afraid that plenty of white boys are dead too, like your son, and plenty of yellow ones too, like the Vietnamese. And you know the Vietnamese didn't want to go. They didn't go. The Viet Cong and all the civilian Vietnamese stayed home and soldiers came from America and killed them."

"Yeah. They did too, but not you. You are right here and my boy is dead."

"Well, Ma'am. I am a draft resister. That means that I did not and will not go. I refuse to serve. You may be familiar with the phrase, 'Hell no, we won't go!' You may have heard that and seen the demonstrations on TV. 'Hey, Hey LBJ, How many kids did you kill today?' Or you may have read about it in the newspapers. 'Hell no, I won't go.' Well, that is what I say. I won't go. (He takes a few beats to let it sink in.) I am sorry that your son went. I wish he was a draft resister too. It would have been easier on him and it would be easier on me. The more resisters, the less pressure to go and fewer soldiers and less killing there would be. There is a choice to make, but not everybody thinks it through. Look at Mohammed Ali."

"Oh, you mean Cassius Clay."

"Yes, Ma'am. You can call him that, but he calls himself Mohammed Ali. He wouldn't go. He gave up his championship and was willing to go to prison because he didn't want to fight in Vietnam and kill people who never called him a...bad name."

"Well, so you can stay home like me and watch the wrestling."

"Yes, Ma'am. I would much rather watch the wrestling. That is something that you and I have in common. I live in Santa Monica near

Muscle Beach. Lots of wrestlers and body builders work-out there. Mr. Universe hangs out there and he is pals with lots of professional wrestlers and other world class body builders. They don't have to go fight either. I don't know why or how, but they stay at the beach and play on the apparatus, like parallel bars, travelling rings, high bars. It is an outdoor gym. I thought it was kind of weird at first, the way they grease up and pose, but these guys are fun to watch. They enjoy volleyball. Not just regular volley ball either, but a game I never saw anywhere else that only men like them can play, I imagine, because it requires their freaky looking oversized muscles."

"Have you ever seen Gorgeous George at the beach?"

"Yes, Ma'am. He is the oldest guy there. He must be fifty."

"Does he still have all his pretty long wavy blond hair and those big beautiful muscles?"

"Yes, Ma'am."

"What about Killer Kowalski and Smasher Sloane?"

"Well, Ma'am. I have only seen them on TV."

"You ever seen the Atomic Skull crusher? "

"Yes, Ma'am. "

"And the Argentine Rocca's backbreaker?

"Yes, Ma'am. That would really hurt. I am glad it is all a big fake."

"Oh, now wait a minute. Don't tell me it's all a fake. I have seen real blood and suffering."

"It must have been an accident. It is show business. It is all a fake."

"You know that?"

"Yes, Ma'am, but I can tell you what is real, and I think you would enjoy knowing it. Those muscle men play volley ball like nobody else. Muscle Volleyball!"

"Muscle Volleyball?"

"Yes, Ma'am. And I have seen Mr. Universe play it with Gorgeous George."

"Muscle Volleyball?"

"Do you know what a 'demi' is?" He strikes a muscle man pose pushing up his bicep backed by his thumb for exaggeration. "Arm demi". He strikes another. "Leg demi", "butt demi".

She starts laughing. "Butt demi? (She covers her smiling mouth with her hands like the 'speak no evil' pose.) "Oh, my goodness, I laughed. I haven't laughed in three months. I haven't left the house and I haven't cracked a smile. (She shakes her head and sighs.) "Oh, my soul. I guess it must be about time." She gives a shrug and little giggle.

"I'm not kidding. They hit the volleyball with their butts tensed up." He mimes it. "Butt demi."

"Butt demi!" She mimes hitting a ball with her butt and laughs.

"Thigh demi" the imaginary game continues and she becomes looser and more comical, laughing and becoming hilarious. Every butt demi is like a running joke that keeps getting bigger.

"Calf demi."

"Butt demi." She falls over the arm of the couch and lands laying on her back and laughs and then she cries, hugging her own shoulders "Oh boy, my boy. They took my boy to Vietnam and killed him. Why did he have to be such a good boy? He could have been a bad boy and stayed home and hung out listening to music and getting high. What kind of trouble could he get into worse than the Army and Vietnam? Do you know he thought the Army would give him an education and a good job? I was afraid for him. I was afraid he would get himself killed. I watched the boys getting killed in Vietnam, but I didn't think it would be him. I saw it all on TV. I thought he would come home and everybody would be so proud. And then he would get a good job. He could have been a TV repairman, or auto mechanic. He could have found a wife to love him. (She sobs.) I don't even know what happened to him over there, but he's dead now and I wish that I had said something to him to make him stay home and stay alive. (Looking up at the ceiling) Oh my boy. I am so sorry. I didn't know it would be you to get killed. I was hoping for so much more. I am so sorry."

"Ma'am, is there anyone else that you might want to give a picture to? Do you have a husband or boyfriend?"

"No." Still crying and trying to pull herself together, she gets off the couch and stands up, straightening her dress. "I'm thirty-five years old and I don't have a husband and I don't have a boyfriend and my son is dead and he is all I had and now I have nobody and nothing. She continues sobbing, dabbing her eyes with a dish towel.

"I am so sorry, Ma'am. I am sorry that Johnny got killed. What is it all for? What a waste."

She sobs louder. "But not you. You can go to the beach and watch all those oily muscle men play volleyball with their butts. It's just not fair. My boy is dead and none of you white boys and muscle men have to fight, except wrestling on TV. Why do all the black boys like my Johnny have to go and fight while all you white boys and muscle men stay home and go to the damned beach. It is not fair. It is just not fair."

"You're right. I agree with you, Ma'am. It's not fair. What about all the Vietnamese getting killed in their own country. They don't even have to join the army to get bombs dropped on them and have their huts burned. How do you think their mothers feel? It must be hell. Their mothers are getting killed too. Our boys are over there now burning huts and killing entire families, destroying rice fields and strafing the farmers and their families from air-planes, bombing their villages with napalm and burning their skin to a blackened crisp. I saw it all on TV too. We are poisoning the crops, defoliating with agent-orange so that they can't hide and fight back. We are starving the ones we don't kill. These are war-crimes. We hung Nazis after World War II for stuff like that. What is the choice if you were born in Vietnam or Laos or Cambodia? They don't come over here to kill us. They just stay home and we come after them. Where can they go? Their country is being destroyed and they have no place to go. We have a choice. We don't have to go. I don't know if your son was a hero or a martyr or just an unlucky young man who didn't know he had an important choice to make; the most important choice of his life. I agree with you. It is not fair. It's not fair for you, not for me, not for your son and not for all the Vietnamese. I really think they would be happy if they could farm some rice and feed their families in peace. I am sorry, but going in the Army and going over there only makes bad things worse for everyone."

"What about you? What are you going to do? Going to prison with your hero Cassius Clay?"

"I don't know what to do. I don't want to go to prison because I want to be free. I am afraid that I might get tortured in prison. Our country has a tradition of abusing draft dodgers and prisoners in general. I can't fight like Mohammad Ali and prison is as scary to me as jungle warfare. I might go to Canada, but it's too cold. Maybe Sweden where they welcome draft resisters too. Maybe I would go to Bolivia and fight like Che Guevara for freedom."

"Che what?"

"Che Guevara? The Argentine rebel revolutionary icon. His poster is on dormitory walls all over America. Castro's best friend?"

"Oh, that Che."

"Yes. That Che. I like what he was doing, taking land from the rich and giving it to the poor. That whole Robin Hood thing appeals to me. I don't think I could join the Sheriff of Nottingham. Given the choice, I would rather fight with Robin Hood. "

"And his merry men? I remember that show."

"Yes, and really, I think I can choose not to fight at all. But if I had to fight, if I was in the Army and sent to Vietnam, I would rather fight with Ho Chi Min."

"Hoochi Coochi Man?"

"I think you are playing with me. You are funny, but really I think Ho Chi Min is more like Robin Hood and Uncle Sam is more like the Sheriff of Nottingham. I really don't understand why it is our business and why any of us Americans would willingly go to the other side of the earth to stop Ho Chi Min from helping his people improve their lives."

"You're saying my son died fighting on the wrong side. You're saying my son died for nothing."

"Worse than that, Ma'am and I don't know exactly what your son did over there or what he was thinking. Maybe he died of a drug overdose or was hit by friendly fire, but our soldiers in Vietnam died killing innocent people in their own homes. I believe that is what Uncle Sam trained them to do and that it is their mission, to terrorize the people, break their will for freedom. We call that winning their hearts and minds. I think that means make them give up their fight for freedom and submit to American military power. We disapprove of redistributing wealth. It is too much like communism. Success in one country, like Cuba or Vietnam might set a good example. Other poor counties might follow. They call it the domino theory."

"Fats Domino?"

"No. Sorry. Not Fats Domino and not Blueberry Hill and not Pork Chop Hill. Our leaders from Truman to Nixon have all been afraid that if one country gets free and chooses something they like to call communism, socialism or something like Robin Hood; it might inspire the same in neighboring countries. Imagine if it got all the way back here in America? Imagine if everybody had a nice place to live, plenty to eat, and great education and health care, like if Johnson had won the war on poverty instead of going whole hog in Vietnam. Rich people are afraid of sharing. It is really sick, but I believe that is what it's about it.

"You got a hell of a nerve. You're telling me my son died fighting on the wrong side."

"Yes, Ma'am.'"

196

"My Johnny was a good boy. He was trying to do what was right."

"Yes, Ma'am, he probably didn't know better. He probably thought he was doing the right thing, but he was ignorant. I guess he was not aware that he had better choices to make. He didn't have to fight and he didn't have to die. What a tragic waste." (She cries. She walks up to the salesman and slaps him hard on the cheek. He doesn't flinch. A few long seconds pass as she burns and he cools. She smacks him on the other. Then she breaks down and cries some more. The salesman stands and watches for a long moment listening to her sob before speaking.)

"Mrs. Johnson. I am sorry. I know that you loved your son and he must have been a wonderful young man. I hate the war and I wish nobody would go and fight it. Then there wouldn't be any dead sons to mourn. I am sorry that I upset you. I am upset too."

"Really?"

"Yes, Ma'am."

"Do you think my son was a hero, or a villain, or just a damned fool?"

"I don't know that. I don't even know what it means to be a hero or a villain anymore. Ho Chi Min is a hero in Vietnam but a villain over here to most of us. Che Guevara is a hero in Bolivia, Peru, most of South America, in Cuba and in Angola, but a villain to most Americans except college students. Mohammad Ali is a hero in prisons and around the world but not in the pentagon. They are my heroes. But they are villains to many patriotic Americans. I'll bet John Wayne hates them all. John Wayne is a hero to most Americans, but he never wore a real uniform except in the movies. He did everything he could to avoid service but he enthusiastically urges boys like me and your son to go over there and kill

197

innocent victims of our anti-communist paranoia. John Wayne's got a hell of a nerve."

"Oh, my. are you a communist?"

"I am not sure what you mean by that, but when I think about communism I think that I don't want to share my toothbrush with anyone, even someone whom I am deeply in love with. You know what I mean. I want some private property and I don't want to stand in line for a roll of toilet paper, like in Russia. I don't think that is what Karl Marx had in mind when he dreamed it up. And I don't want to eat my rice one grain at a time, starving like the children in China did during their great famine in the fifties. And I don't mind working to make a buck to pay my bills. But I wouldn't want to be delivering bullets and napalm bombs to Vietnam to make war profiteers richer and put common people into a state of terror and misery. I'd rather deliver pizza and chicken to hungry pot-heads at UCLA.

Do you think that Germans who grieve their fathers, uncles, cousins and sons who died wearing Nazi uniforms think that they were heroes? Do you think German soldiers were killing Russians because they hated Communism and Americans because they hated Capitalism? Did they kill French because they ate snails and Brits because their sports cars were unreliable? Do you think they were more philosophical than your son? Did your son hate Communism or was he hoping for a better education after the war, a better job and a better life? Communism, Capitalism, Fascism? How about Imperialism? Do soldiers kill and die because of political and economic philosophy? My uncle Joe tramped all over North Africa and up through Italy carrying a gun and bayonet during World War

198

II. He told me what mattered to him the most in his years as a soldier at war was dry feet and something warm to eat. When I was a little boy I was impressed with his war experience and asked him to tell me about it. He didn't like talking about the army and the war.

Uncle Joe was a Russian Jewish immigrant, as a boy, an undistinguished student, a Coney Island lifeguard before the war and a mailman for about thirty years after. He had three jobs all working for the government and a secure old age. He was a union man and he was proud to be a civil servant. He paid his dues and enjoyed all the privileges that this country and FDR afforded him. He was a registered Democrat, but I don't think it would be accurate to call him a capitalist. He was a soldier, but not an imperialist, or a fascist, or a communist. He was a voter. He was also a handball player, a golfer, and a terrific swimmer. My uncle was a nice guy and that defined him for me and that is what I want to be; a nice guy. I want to skip the war and be a nice guy. I think most soldiers just want to stay alive and come home."

"You said a mouthful, young man."

"Yes Ma'am. You got me going here, lady. I hope you're not still sore with me."

(She shakes her head again and gives a slight smile) "You got me going too, son."

"You're going to meet someone and you are going to be happy again. You are good looking and great at muscle- volleyball, and you have a lot of passion." (He pats his own cheeks and smiles while she looks at him, seeming to smell him again.   She smiles and flexes her arms and shoulders.) "Maybe you will meet a veteran, or a man who needs someone to love and wants to love someone like you. There are plenty like that."

"You know that?"

"Yes Ma'am."

"Well, (she sniffles) you are nice. I must look like hell."

"You look beautiful. I think crying becomes you in a sad and beautiful way. Very sad and very beautiful and true."

"Really?"

"Really."

"You are a sweet boy." She smiles and reaches out. They hug for a moment holding each other's shoulders with faces cheek to cheek. They release and stand close holding each other at elbow length and looking into each other's eyes.

"Don't hurt me." He says, just kidding, and she kisses his cheek.

"Other side." He says turning his cheek. She smiles and kisses his other cheek.

"I am sorry I slapped you, but you got a hell of a nerve. You're lucky I didn't hurt your worse. You sure hurt me." He reciprocates kissing both her cheeks, like a European.

"Ma'am, you won a prize today and I hope that you can collect it, because someday soon you are going to meet someone and you are going to want to give him a beautiful portrait to admire when you can't be together; a full color professional 5 X 7 portrait like this." He holds up the picture for her to see again. "Which would be more convenient for your photo session, Tuesday or Friday?"

"Oh, I think Friday."

"Morning or afternoon?"

"Afternoon. Would 3PM be OK?"

"3PM, next Friday afternoon. You have an appointment. Mrs. Johnson. They require a $2 deposit which is 100% refundable when Frank Williams arrives here to photograph you. They require the deposit to make sure that someone is here after Frank comes all the way from Hollywood with his equipment. If you don't have $2, they would accept a book of Blue Chip trading stamps."

"Oh no, I'm not giving up my trading stamps. I am saving up for a trip to Hawaii."

"Well, OK. Then they need $2. Please give me $2 now and you can keep the appointment."

She reaches into a change purse that she had in the front pocket in the apron of her dress and pulls out a couple of folded up bills, counting out two. She puts it in his hand, closing his fingers around it and holds his hand like a mother might after giving her young son milk money. He puts the money in his hip pocket and hands her a receipt. "Thank you, Mrs. Johnson."

"Thank you, son."

(Lights fade to dim and black…curtain closes. Cornet resumes playing the slow blues, small motorcycle revs.)

JUST SAY NO

When it came my time to serve in Vietnam, I resisted. The draft board did not deem me as a conscientious objector. Truancy had ruined my student deferment. My trick knee wasn't tricky enough, my bad back was really OK and mega-doses of LSD left me fit to serve. With half a million troops in Vietnam, selective service was scraping the bottom of the barrel. On a sunny spring day in 1969 I passed my physical with flying colors, classified 1A. I had the right stuff.

During the next thirty months I entered many appeals for deferment and they were all rejected. While I wished for the end of war, I contemplated my choices; jungle warfare, prison, exile, life on the lam, underground. When the draft lottery was announced I took my chance. My number was 212 and they only called up to 195. It was December 1971 when I realized that I was free. I had won the draft lottery. It was cause to celebrate. On a snowy night during intercession at LIU Post, I went to a party and impulsively decided that I needed a trip to the beach. "Who wants to go to the beach?" I asked.

"Wow. Hey. It's too cold for the beach, man." said Sam. He had a trimmed light brown beard, wore tailored jeans and had a haircut that resembled Prince Edward's.

"Not Jones Beach, man, I mean like some place tropical."

"Like Hawaii?"

"Yeah, like Hawaii, but maybe somewhere closer, like Jamaica."

"Yeah, Jamaica."

The idea gained traction. Twenty minutes later my new best friend, Sam and I were going back to our dorm rooms to gather supplies. With borrowed tent, sleeping bags, and backpacks stuffed with bare necessities, we took a snowy ride to Kennedy Airport. Oh, we did manage to stash hashish and LSD into our tent poles and were delighted with ourselves at being so clever and deceptive.

At the ticket counter we learned that the only tropical place we could escape to that night would be Nassau, so we bought a couple tickets and went. We got to Paradise Island and started to pitch our tent, but police rousted us and made us book a hotel room. At the hotel we met a bunch of Australian youths and followed them to the City Bar. As we groused about the police, the overdeveloped resort, our crappy hotel and the expensive beer, a wild man came barreling across the room towards us. He was bare-chested, built like Tarzan but disheveled; his long hair and beard tangled and snagged with ripped leaves and vines.

"Hey mate. Have a beer?" Said an Aussie.

"Yah. Thank you." The wild man sounded like Chris Lloyd.

The bartender brought us more beers and we gave one to our guest. "Where you been mate?"

After drinking half the bottle with one gulp, he took a couple of deep breaths and drained the rest. His eyes were open wide and his jaw was dropped so low, it looked as though he was in shock. His skin was sunburned and his eyes resembled a spooked horse's. He belched, swallowed and uttered in a choked whisper. "Eleuthra."

A short blond haired Aussie with blood shot eyes said, "What's that mate?"

"Eleuthra…Eleuthra…it's an island paradise with mangos and coconuts, there for the taking. Everything is free." As he described his lost paradise he downed a double Gregory Brother's Dark Rum and another Red Label Beer. His countenance took on a healthy glow and our party became enthralled.

"How would a bloke get to this Eleuthra?" asked Sam. He had taken on the Australian accent and a new attitude. He affected a stiff upper lip. Nobody paid attention to this transformation, but I found it amusing and more to the point, he had asked an excellent question.

"Go to the graveyard and ask for Doc Holliday." We all looked at each other. This was getting crazy, but paradise awaited.

"Where would the graveyard be located, mate?" Sam was continuing the interview in character and quite pleased with himself. We nodded to each other in approval, like Laurel and Hardy.

After a bit of conversation the Australians paid the bar bill and we went back to our cruddy hotel to gather our gear before the search for Doc Holliday. We walked in the tropical night invigorated with the sea-breeze. As we passed the commercial district, we found the bone-yard ahead. The ancient graves were stacked above ground and we became giddy with adventure. I played a sea shanty on my Hohner "C" harp and we danced a frolicking jig with our friends high up on the graves. Doc Holliday found us. He was a handsome young Bahamian with puka beads, dress slacks, and a big Afro. He didn't smile and I noticed that he was hiding some bad teeth. He looked like he had a toothache. "Yas got to take da mailboat for Eleuthra."

"How would we find that?" Sam asked. He was in his aspect of David Niven.

"Gimme $5 and I will take you to Barabbas."

"Barabbas?" said a tall thin brown haired Australian. *I didn't like the sound of it either.*

"Yah, man, Barabbas. He know the Portuguese captain uh da boat. He take you dere."

So we walked down to the rotting pier section of an ancient marina. Doc disappeared for a few minutes. He came back with a solid looking youth who had matted hair. Beneath a shrunken turquoise tee-shirt with a sequined flamingo his pudgy tummy protruded over the waistband of his tight jeans.

"You must be Barabbas, Yah?" Sam was incorrigible.

"Yah. I be Barabbas man. You want da mailboat?"

Soon we were on board an old wooden boat with a Christmas Tree on deck. It was lit up with a single string of white bulbs. It was Christmas Eve. We seven night-trippers were traveling for a low fee, which did not include privileges below deck. The captain, a portly, middle aged man of few words, had himself a Christmas Eve dinner and did not share. We could smell the fish frying. We were feeling hungry and cold, but kept warm by dancing and making music on deck. Sam and the Australians enjoyed my shanties in the graveyard and on deck they became enthusiastic fans of my blues harp. Sam took particular delight in a sound I produced that prompted him to dance something resembling the "Funky Chicken", with his head down, shoulders hunched and elbows sticking out like wings.

Before dawn the boat reached port and we departed into the darkness. We walked in weary, silent, single-file on a sandy road until a pickup truck pulled over and gave us a ride to Surfers Beach. Somehow, I had been out of the loop, but that was apparently the planned destination of our Aussie friends.

On the beach at last, Sam and I discovered that neither of us had ever earned any boy-scout merit badges. We struggled with our tent. In exhaustion we decided to just open our sleeping bags on the sand and enjoy the stars. But we were cold, so we tried to build a fire. Even this became a trial. We had enough dried palm fronds and crinkly leaves, but the breeze kept blowing out our matches. I leaned into our little sand-pit lined with stones and blew lightly trying to spread our feeble little flame. Sam's eyes looked forlorn. His great charm and sense of adventure had worn thin. We had been partying day and night and needed to crash. We were cold, tired and alone in the wilderness, or so it seemed. As I gently blew there was an astonishing flash of fire. My eyebrows were singed and it smelled like fried ants. The fire was roaring. Flames were dancing like savages. In its orange light I looked up first at Sam's revitalized face and then saw that we were surrounded by naked people. They were laughing at us. We were laughing too. We were saved.

But who were these people? I wondered. They made us laugh so hard. We told them we were from NY and a thin bearded young man who was a few years older than us took us on a verbal trip around NY via public transportation that peaked somewhere in Queens. I think he was gay. We smoked a joint with them. They were all so funny. They had us literally rolling in laughter. We were holding our ribs and tears were blurring our vision. They told us if we needed anything they were staying in tents away from the beach near where the bluffs rose up to steep limestone cliffs. Exhausted we fell asleep by the warm fire.

In the morning I felt a cool wet sensation on my feet and it rose to my ankles. I tried to go back to sleep. I heard a sloshing sound and the sensation increased, sopping my sleeping bag and cooling me up to my knees. When a wave wet my face and left me coughing salt water I woke up and realized that the rising tide had reached us. But Sam and I were feeling good natured from the smoky treat as we cursed and gathered our wet belongings. We retreated to our new friends' camp and found them sleeping. We settled nearby and were grateful when the sun gained altitude. We dried out and snoozed in the shade of a coconut palm.

We woke to the smell of broiling shell fish and the sound of merry conversation. Jimmy Flowers and his companion Heather had joined the Fire-Sign Theater. That is what they called themselves. They also claimed that they were University of Chicago grad students on the lamb, running up charges on a stolen American Express credit card. Jimmy was a wiry Navy veteran. He and his pretty stewardess girl-friend were at the beach with an AWOL Navy buddy named Dirk who was an expert spear fisherman. So we had plenty of Bahamian lobster which had no claws and red snapper. Sam and I went to forage and discovered that the shipwrecked sailor we met at the City Bar in Nassau was right. Eleuthera was a virtual Garden of Eden with bananas, mangos, coconuts, and pineapples in abundance for us to gather by the armful. We rejoined our friends and felt like full partners in the feast.

The Fire-Sign Theater shared our hashish and LSD. We shared their MDA. That was a powder that we sniffed like cocaine. I was hesitant because I had never heard of it. They assured me that it was not speed but was more like LSD without the sci-fi edge. I discovered that it gave our island paradise a rosy hue and it gave me a deep appreciation for the subtle percussive counterpoint of heart and lungs, circulation and respiration, feeling of one with our environment; the rhythm of the island, its sweet, salty breeze and the gentle lapping of its surf. It was in my blood.

My companions were my new best friends. Jimmy showed me how to make monkey rum with a coconut and a few raisons. We buried it in the sand to ferment. Dirk showed me how to snorkel. Our beach was protected by a coral reef. Under water I discovered another world of awesome color and an entire ecosystem of flora and fauna which were to my untrained eyes and expanded vision at times indistinguishable. I wandered underwater. Tiny fish kissed my skin as I cruised with barracudas unafraid. Looking deep into an inviting crevice expecting to find a luminous angel fish, I found instead the yellow eyes of a moray eel. As it exited its hiding place, I nearly bit off the mouthpiece of my snorkel and rocketed to the surface. I was terrified and then grateful to be all of one piece when I returned to the warm beach. I felt safer swimming, body surfing, and crashing on the soft pink sand.

We set up camp in a coral cave that we discovered by climbing the cliff. Inside was a natural chimney so we were warm at night with a driftwood fire. Our friends moved in next store, with Jimmy and Heather a bit further down in another spacious cave. We developed a taste for the abundant MDA and sniffed days and nights and then our small party was expanded. The Australians had disappeared the first night and we wondered if they had been just an hallucination, but they returned on New Year's Eve when we were joined by a larger group all of whom carried surf boards. The parade of new comers continued all day until there were at least thirty surfers doing acrobatic tricks in the high tide.

Sam and I resumed our fake Aussie accents, mispronouncing all the vowels. We cracked each other up as the goof continued because our pals from down-under found nothing stranger about our fake accents than they did with our New York accents. The Fire-Sign Theater joined our improvisation and they were experts. Jimmy kept his southern twang and Heather proved to be one of our biggest fans. I had a bit of a crush on her, but kept it to myself. I actually found myself missing an old girl-friend. It was a delayed grief. I had broken up with her to spare her any harm that might befall her as my partner. *Was it paranoia?* I believed that as a draft resister and self-styled revolutionary, my fascist enemies might use my girl-friend to hurt me, either by hurting her, or by using her to bait me into a more vulnerable location. My future had been so uncertain, and I cut myself loose from the most solid and nurturing emotional relationship I had ever known. I broke her heart. She didn't understand. "Why do you have to be so crazy?" she said through her tears. I held her and we pressed our bodies together while I cried with her. What I learned much later was that when I broke her heart, I broke my own too. But, at Surfers' Beach, in Eleuthera, Heather's contagious laughter was haunting as it made me long for a girl and a love that I did not understand I was missing. *Why was I laughing and crying at the same time?* Heather could see me and read my emotions. She could hold me and comfort me, but it did not heal my soul. She wasn't Lisa, who I left behind. Nobody got me like she did. I looked at the surf as it crashed on the sand. It receded in thin white foamy rivulets that undulated into forms resembling script, spelling out the illegible answers to my frustrated quandary, *why was I crying?*

The feasts continued and the party grew into a festival. Sam and I routinely foraged with great success until we were informed that there was bread in Gregorytown. So we walked farther seeking the staff of life. We hadn't brought anything to drink and the arid climate made us thirsty. We satisfied ourselves with fresh fruit along the way, mostly mangos. We saw a crippled man sitting by the side of the dirt road. "Is this the way to Gregorytown?" I asked.

"Ya Man. Gregorytown." He waved his arm down the road. We noticed an ugly scar across his calf.

Farther on we found another man sitting with a similar scar. He too waved us toward our destination. The east side of the road was covered with pineapples, more than we had seen before, and no other fruits, just many acres of pineapples which must have been cultivated. The west side of the road was barren and sandy with an occasional coconut palm here and an aloe plant there.

We got to town and were happy to see children playing. They were teasing a goose. A little girl in a yellow dress leaned toward it, bent at the waist, waggled her tongue and shook her head. When he hissed back she ran along with the other children and the goose chasing their behinds. Then a little boy with a Dodger cap on backward, took big goofy steps in slow motion toward the goose until he caused another chase. Sam had a sailor's hat turned inside out, a purple and black Procol Harum tee-shirt,

210

black speedo bathing suit and tennis shoes without socks. He looked at the goose and the goose looked at him. The goose stretched his neck and lowered his head. Sam did the same. The goose hissed and so did Sam. The goose moved his head forward and back. It looked like part of a dance I had seen on Soul Train. Sam did the same. The goose waddled away and Sam duplicated its gate chasing the goose which delighted the children. "Da Gooseman. Da Gooseman!" They hollered and laughed. Sam was pleased with the attention and continued to play goose as the children danced around him. "Are you da Gooseman?" A little girl asked.

"Ya." He was imitating their accent now. "I da Gooseman."

The village had low buildings, their pastel paint faded to light yellow, orange and blue. Sun drenched it like an overexposed darkroom negative, dreamlike and surreal. I heard a tinny recording of James Brown singing "Papa's Got a Brand New Bag". Women shaking wash and hanging it between their houses, children scampering and playing, everybody seemed to have the same music in their bodies. It was the rhythm of the island and it was James Brown combined. It was a soulful ballet in paradise. We continued through the parched street until we smelled bread. We bought a few yeasty loaves from a smiling lady who laughed and gave us change. "Thank you, Mama!" I said. Sam just nodded his head and continued to waddle.

"Ya be careful darlings. Da sun be so hot." She called after us. We continued into the village. There were women selling fresh fish, and there was a fruit stand. We had been eating everything for free, but here it was all for sale in the village.

We found a surfer's hostel, like a big dormitory. We looked inside and it was empty except for about fifteen double bunks and a lot of luggage crowding the floor. A skinny old black man greeted us. "Ya boys is too late. Come back tomorrow."

"Our friends are staying here. They are down at the beach surfing. We just came for provisions."

"Ya got da bread. Bahama Mama be frying fish at noon. It nice."

"Thank you."

"Dat nice, man. And you be wanting some fruit."

"We have plenty of fruit. We have been finding it right near where we are camped."

"You finding it?"

"Ya man." said Sam in his native aspect. "Eet growing wild like da Garden of Eden."

"Da Gregory Brothers better not catch you stealing they fruit or they cut your legs with da machete and you never walk away wit dere fruit no more."

He wasn't smiling, just looking at Sam. Sam wasn't smiling and wasn't talking anymore. We were remembering the crippled men that we had seen along the road.

"Maybe we'll buy some fruit while we are here." I suggested.

"Dat right smart."

There was something about this old man that I liked. "You boys come wit me and meet the bossman."

Soon we were at the source of the James Brown music that had progressed to "It's a Man's World".

212

"Hey boss. We got new friends."

"Well, who the hell is here?"

"We got us new friends."

A chubby red faced man with a clean straw fedora and a long cigar came out to the shady porch. He was followed by a slim white lady who resembled Cher, but with short hair. She wore a blue leather mini-skirt and stiletto heels with dark stockings. Her bare midriff was tickled by a short fringed vest that focused our attention on her otherwise modest cleavage. I'm "Fat Daddy and this here is Sister Sue. You already met Saint James." A handsome young man with long wavy blond hair slipped into the room and stood close to Sue. "And this here is Tim. Who are you boys and what's your business here?" He gave Sam a hard look and then shook his head and pressed his lips without talking. Sam did a goosey head nod. "Your friend's been out in the sun too long. I can tell you that."

"We are here vacationing at Surfer's Beach and came to town for bread."

"Sue. Bring these boys some lemonade. Or would you like something stronger?" Fat Daddy lifted his left leg and made a gesture like he was pulling an old fashioned train's air horn. He made a loud fart. "There now. It don't get any better if you hold it in." He chuckled and looked around. "Go on and get some lemonade, God Dammit. Now you boys got names I suppose."

"I am Steve and this is Sam."

"Gooseman" said Sam.

"Gooseman" said Fat Daddy. "I should have guessed."

213

Tim lit a joint and we passed it around. Sue came in and shared it too. I felt so comfortable with these people.

"How long you boys planning to stay on our fair island?" said Fat Daddy.

"I don't know." *I didn't even know how long we had been there and hadn't given any thought to the subject of time.*

"Don't know? Hell. Don't you boys have tickets to return or can we expect you boys to be our new friends in the neighborhood? This place doesn't look like much now, but just you wait. I'm a land developer. Me and the Gregory Brothers have big plans for this place. You won't recognize it in a few years. But you must have something that you do besides walk like a silly goose." He was looking at Sam. Sam walked around the room in his goose walk giving the funky chicken elbow gesture in time to James Brown. The tape was up to "Cold Sweat". Sam had rhythm. He might have been nuts, but he could sure do the funky chicken.

"We are students." I volunteered. "We go to school in NY. We are on intercession."

We stayed there all afternoon, sipping lemonade and later Planter's Punch. I was rocking drunk and we all danced with Sue who entertained us like a GoGo Girl. Saint James brought us plates of fried conch and grilled pineapples. We even had some salad with lemon and pepper dressing. Tim and I had a philosophical discussion about fame, fortune, and political ambition. He concluded that none of it was worth seeking; that it would just happen as fate and probably none of it was worth having.

It got dark and Fat Daddy told Saint James to look at the moon. "Read the boys the date with Sue's stockings. Go on Sue. Take off one of them

214

pretty stockings so that James can tell the date for our guests." Sue sat back on a rattan chair with a shiny blue cushion, unclipped her garters and slid her stocking off. James pulled it tight across his face. His nose, lips, and kinky hair were all flattened as he looked up at the crescent moon. "Now how many stiches can you count across the fattest part of the moon?"

"It is four, five, six, seven, eight, nine." said Saint James.

"January ninth." said Fat Daddy.

"Wow. I can't believe it. We have been here for more than two weeks."

"Well if you boys decide to go back to Nassau, the mail boat comes once a week. Hey, Saint James. Why not drive the boys to the beach. I don't think they want to walk that far."

Saint James drove us in a vintage Cadillac and he played James Brown on the eight track all the way. By car it only took a few songs. When we got there James Brown was singing "I Got The Feelin."

We returned to the beach with bread, but no fruit. We had missed dinner but nobody cared.

Forty years later, I asked my nonagenarian father if he remembered how we got back. "Well, your dear old mother prevailed upon me to wire you just enough money for the return trip. If it was just up to me you might have been left stranded, but your mother wanted you to come home."

I got back just in time and took a share in a group house on the beach in Asharoken. But Sam did not return and I never heard from him again.

215

WHEN CHESTER COMES MARCHING HOME

Part of my job over four decades has involved managing sales specialists and product demonstrators in stores like Macys and Bloomingdales. I would go to the stores to meet, train and supervise. Drawing from NY's vast pool of talent I have hired some impressive people to perform the tasks required to educate the public. This case involved proper use, care, and especially sharpening of cutlery.

Chester worked as a selling specialist for Cuisinarts in Bloomingdales for ten years. After that he worked for Henckels Cutlery for ten more, first in Bloomingdales and later in Macys. We became friendly over the years. He was a dapper gentleman, and we were born in the same year. He remained physically fit and was as graceful as a Kung Fu Master. I admired his clear diction and precise vocabulary. He was diplomatic with co-workers, a natural leader, and a "go-to guy" on the selling floors. He often helped me with merchandising challenges, even before we worked together officially. He talked us past recalcitrant union stewards and guided me through the vast sub-basement in Macy's where steam hissed and rats splashed through dark, fetid puddles, as we searched for misplaced inventory.

When he was fired, I found him and commiserated. They had discontinued his contract because he was too familiar with a female co-worker. I knew her and while I could understand his attraction to her, he had apparently made her uncomfortable enough to complain. Bloomingdales deserves credit for responding to protect her. Were they unfair to Chester? It was to my thinking, a sensitive issue.

He told me that this was the second time he had a complaint of this nature. I paused to reconsider our friendship. My observations were that he was a lady's man, which is not necessarily a bad thing. Ladies seemed to respond to him in a pleasant way. They seemed flattered by his attention. He was chivalrous. It is unfortunate that he made a lady or two uncomfortable. He suffered from it, without making any disparaging remarks about either of the women involved. To me that was further evidence that he was a gentleman and that his attention was unappreciated and misunderstood.

At my suggestion, we met for lunch at the Grill in Macy's Cellar. We drank beer, ate well, rehashed the complaints, and got to know each other better.

Chester grew up in Newark, NJ. He was a gifted athlete and scholar, with nearly perfect SAT scores. I noticed that he spoke like a well written book, but not pedantic or pretentious in any way. "Chester, you are one of the smartest people I know." I had to tell him. He nodded in appreciation and told me that he was recruited by many colleges and chose University of Ohio because it was outside of Newark. He did not want to live at home. The other reason he chose Ohio was that it had the largest undergrad population with the highest proportion of females.

"How many young women can one man date?" I asked him and laughed. He did not answer, but nodded and smiled until I stopped laughing.

It was Vietnam era, when demand for military personnel was at its peak. Roger was recruited again. This time Uncle Sam wanted him. He came from a modest economic background and was seduced by a full scholarship including grad school. He stayed in school as long as he could and received more than one advanced degree in art.

He had stayed in school long enough to wait out Vietnam. He thought he had beaten the system, but when he left campus he was obligated to serve. He became an Army Ranger, received special training and became expert in jungle warfare.

Chester was assigned to Central America. He never met Ronald Regan, Admiral Poindexter and Oliver North, but he helped their Contras resist leftist rebels. As part of his duty, he was required to supervise Nicaraguan soldiers. During interrogations they made the suspected rebels watch while they raped, tortured, mutilated and murdered their children in front of their wives, and then the wives, before doing much the same to the suspects. He told me about it in as much detail as I could stand. We did not cry together, but we stopped talking. In the busy restaurant, we were silent. We were moved and close to tears looking across the table at each other. Our hearts were in our throats. After a long pause and another sip of beer, he said, "After you see something like that, you don't forget it."

This helped me understand why a man of Chester's ability was happy to have an easy job working in department stores where he could meet lots of stylish women. We finished our beer. Art was Chester's other passion. He taught disadvantaged children in Newark and even paid for their art supplies. Although not a billionaire like our erstwhile mayor, Mike Bloomberg, Roger was single, straight, liked women and had a social conscience.

I hired Roger and he worked under my supervision for ten years, into his sixties. His reports were hand-written because he had not developed computer skills. I had some complaints from my clients that his reports were "unprofessional" because they were not communicated electronically. I converted them to emails. I admired his penmanship. It had an artistic quality to it, like calligraphy. I appreciated the quality of his reports. His observations were insightful. The content was valuable. Sales were strong. He was an effective employee.

One day, I noticed that he was limping. I didn't know it, but he often hiked from his home in Newark to Macy's. That is four hours each way to work for a four hour shift that paid a hundred dollars plus expenses. He did it to save money as I paid him an allowance for the cost of transportation, and he enjoyed the exercise. A car had run over his foot and he walked anyway. That day I drove him home. Listening to Charles Mingus and discussing ensemble music, we enjoyed the luxurious ride. He directed me to the neat row house that he shared with his aging father, who was also a decorated veteran. Their home was in a government sponsored development which sat like an island of thirty decent clustered townhouses in a neighborhood so depressed and desolate, that I was afraid when I left him that I might get car-jacked.

I had another complaint. This time it was from Macys that he was wearing his "colors" to work. He had some decorations for bravery that he liked to wear. He refused to remove his medals and ribbons. Chester was better dressed than his fellows, and refused to comply with their dress-code. I appealed to the manager, who was usually reasonable. I explained that Chester was a decorated hero and that we were lucky to have a veteran of his caliber. The appeal was denied.

After Chester's father died, I had trouble reaching him on the phone for assignments and his reports became erratic. All his contact information was changing so often that I could not reach him to discuss work. It went on for months. I would just go to Macy's to see him. He was charming and affable as always.

Without a reliable phone number, email, or mailing address he was unmanageable. I fired him. He continued sending in useless late reports. The president of my client's company was a Vietnam veteran whom I had made aware of Chester's service. To his credit, he kept paying until I could make the break abundantly clear.

Chester was sixty-six when he was last seen leaving Macys. He was wearing his uniform and medals with pride. They wouldn't let him work; not like that. I can see him now, limping along the Pulaski Skyway, breathing rush-hour exhaust fumes and burnt rubber smoke, high above the eternally smoldering underground wetland fires, an unarmed, gray-haired Army Ranger.

CPSIA information can be obtained
at www.ICGtesting.com
Printed in the USA
LVHW021223071019
633402LV00002B/427/P